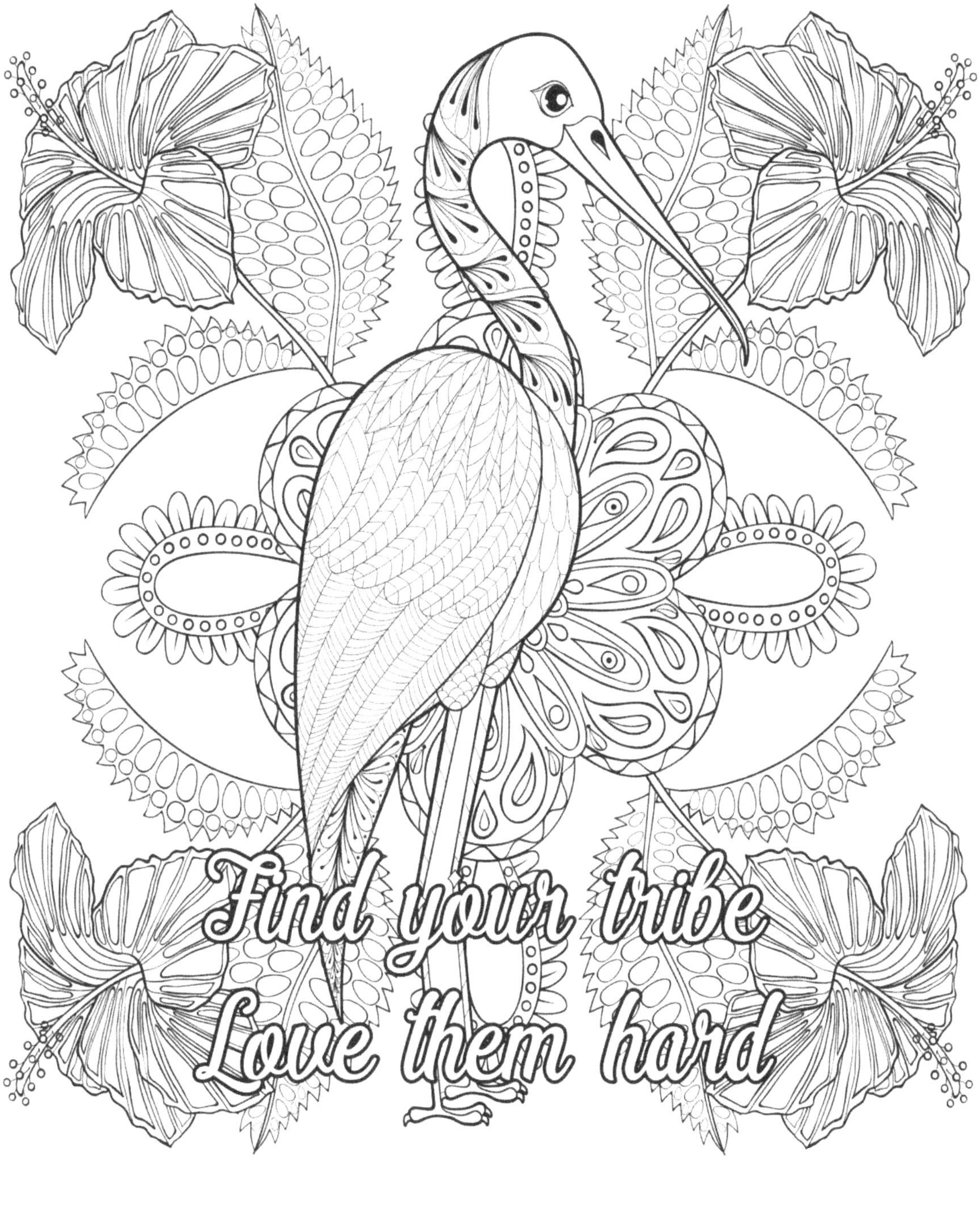

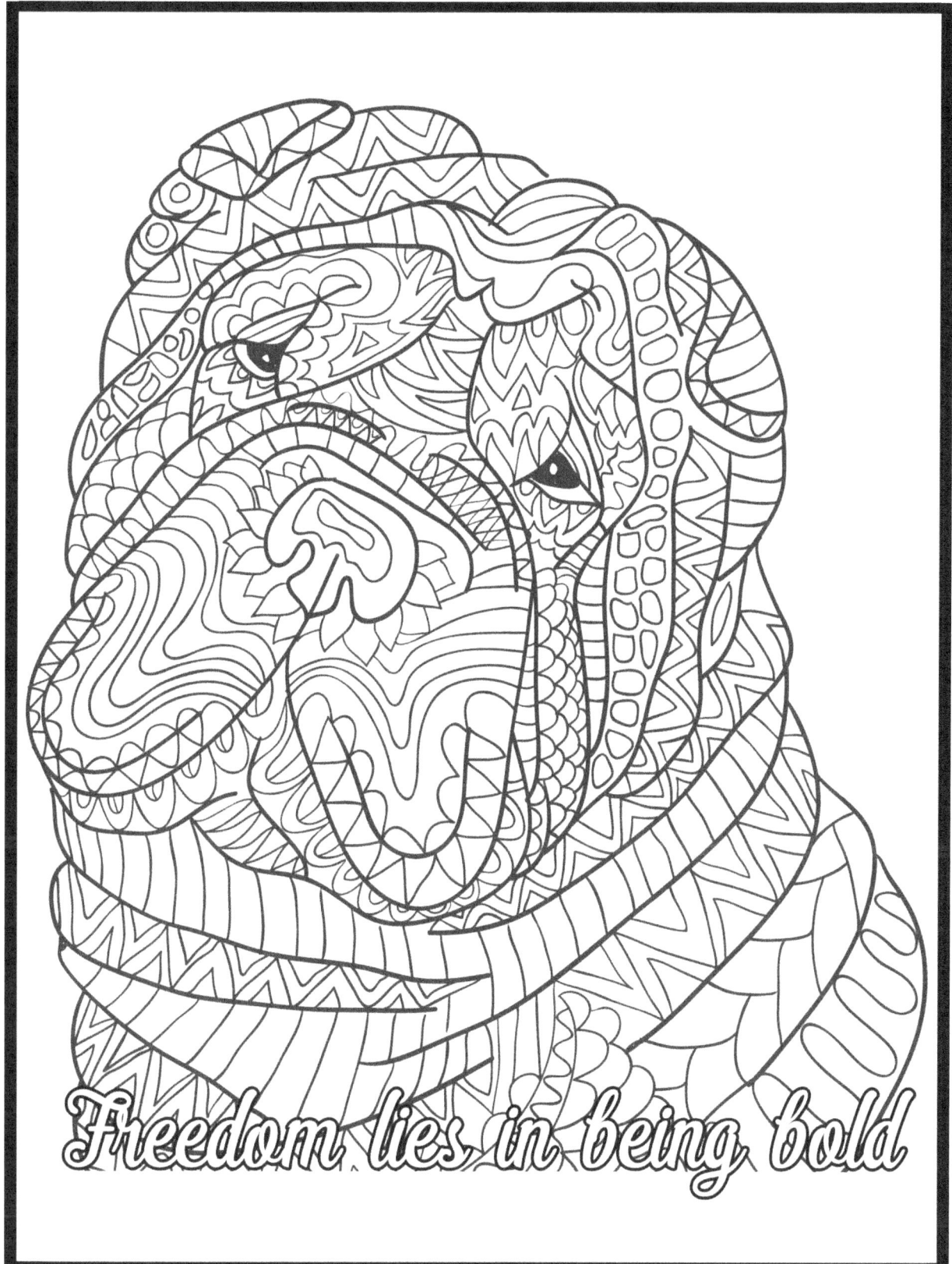

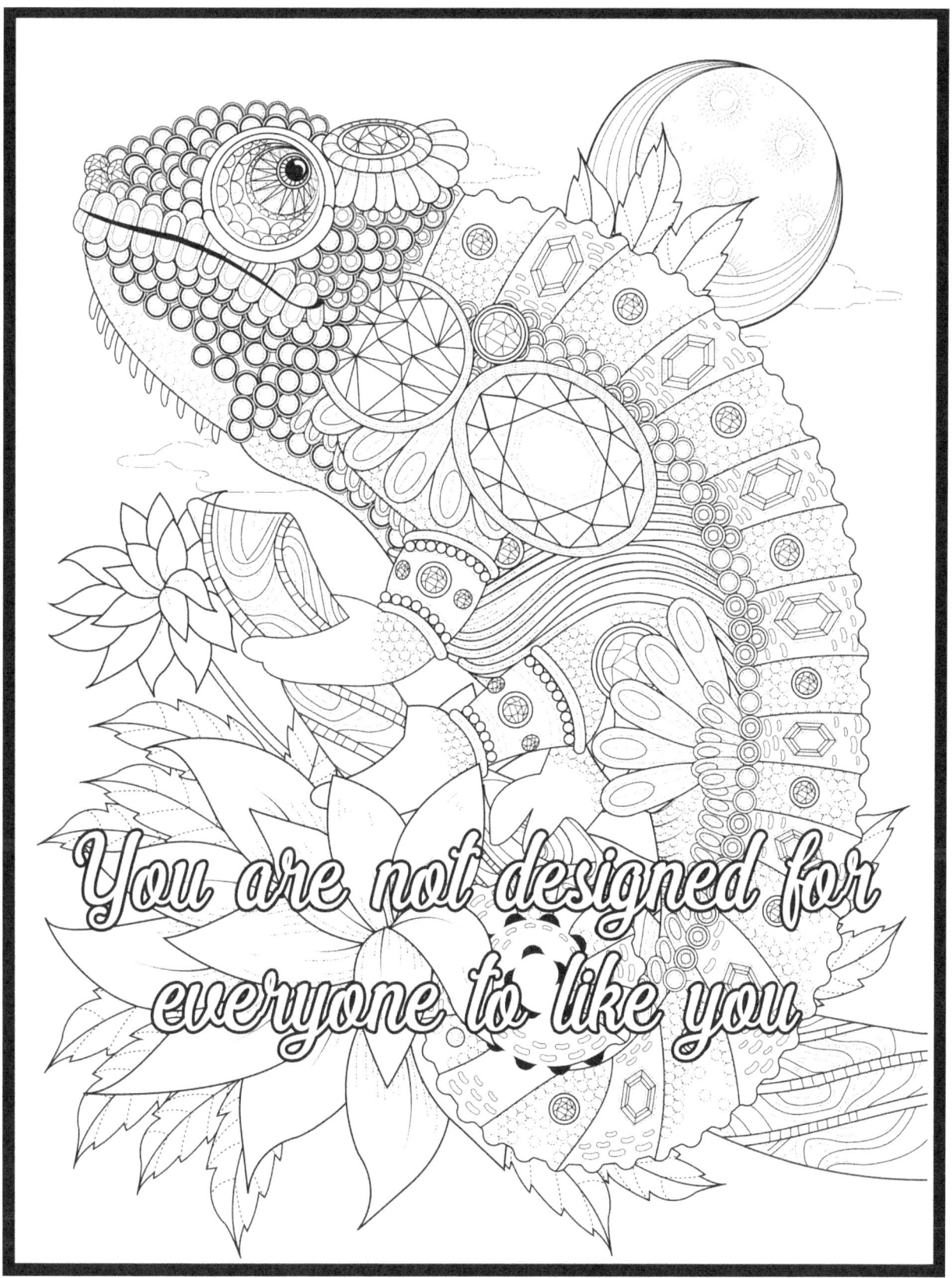

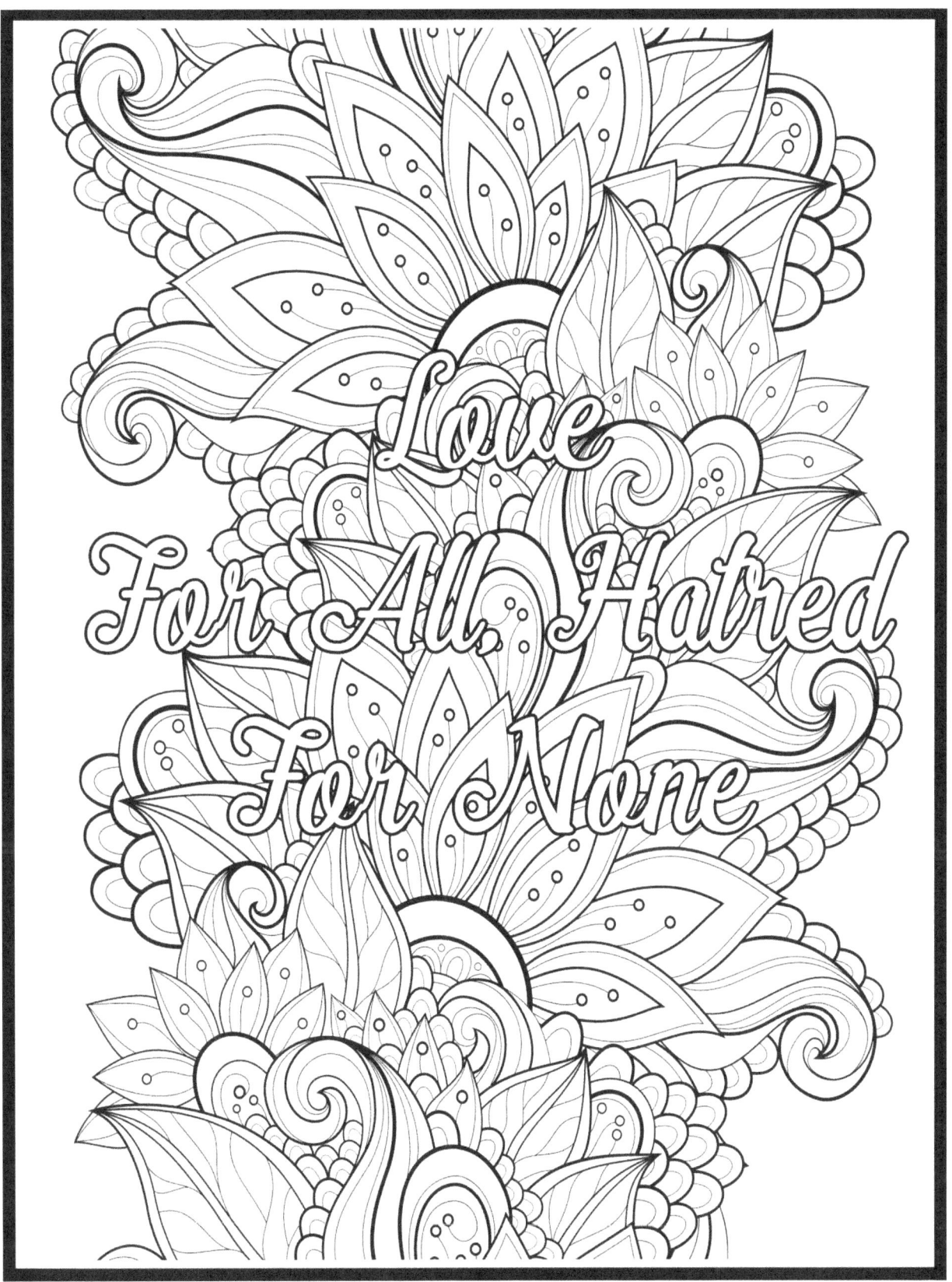

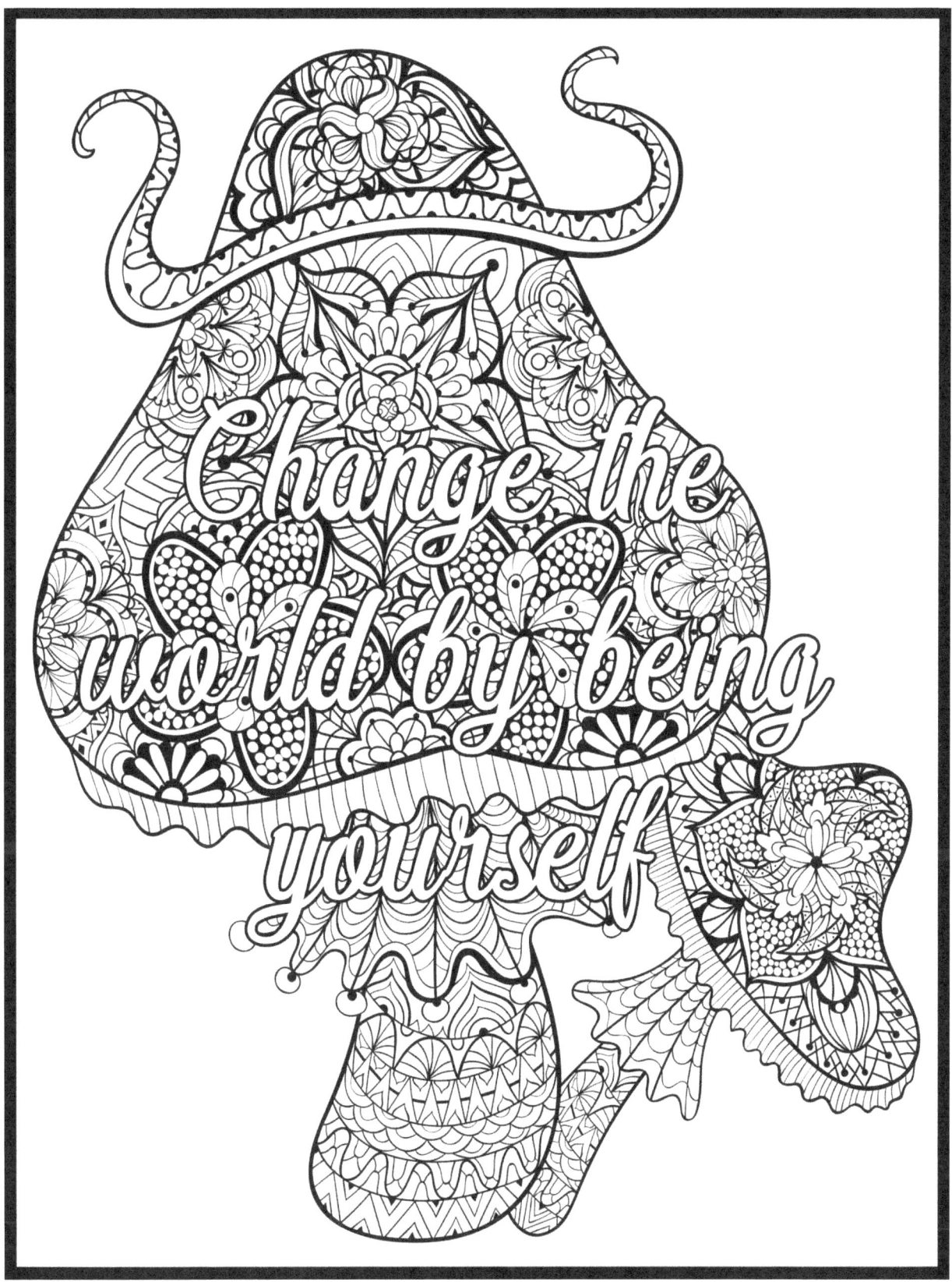

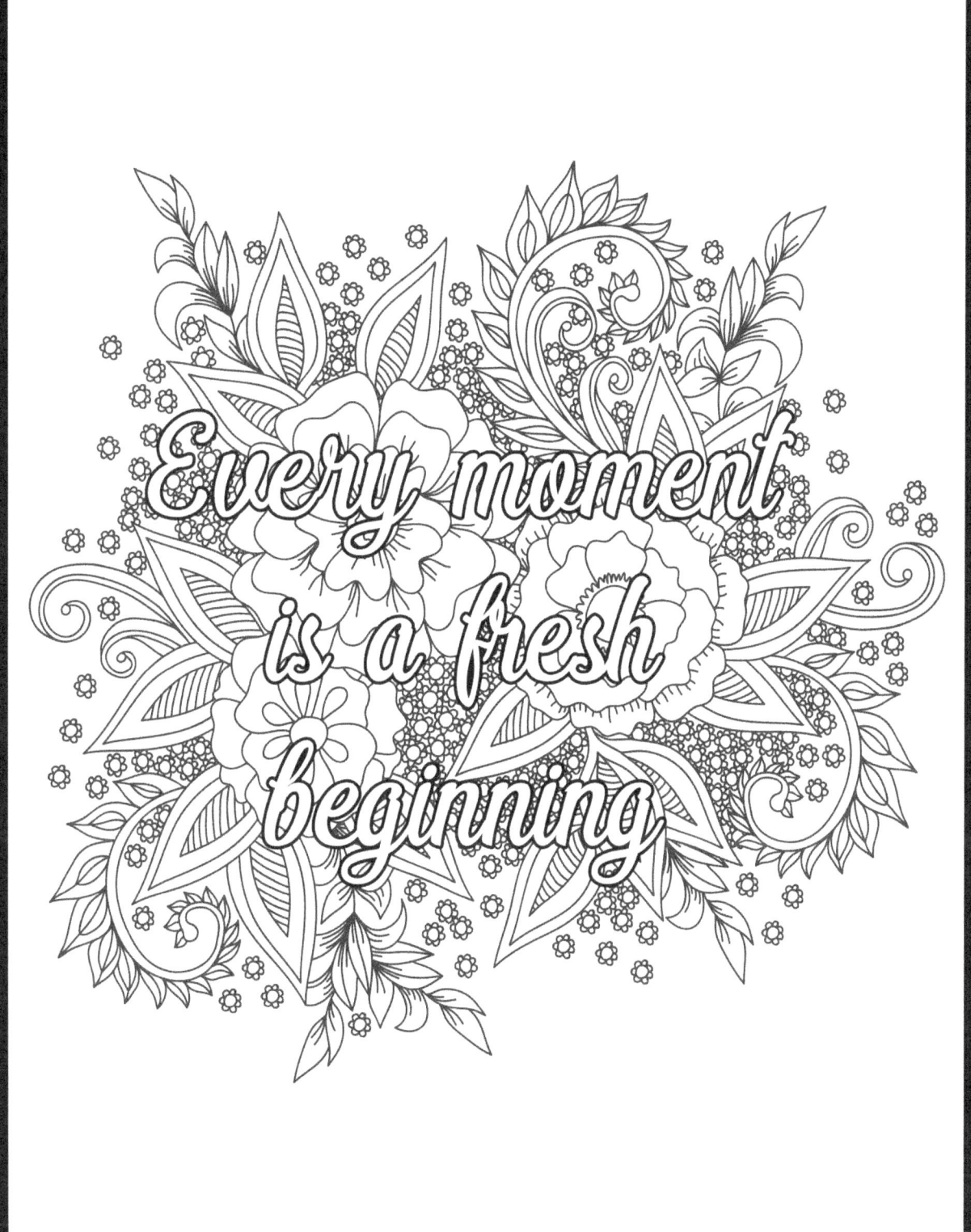

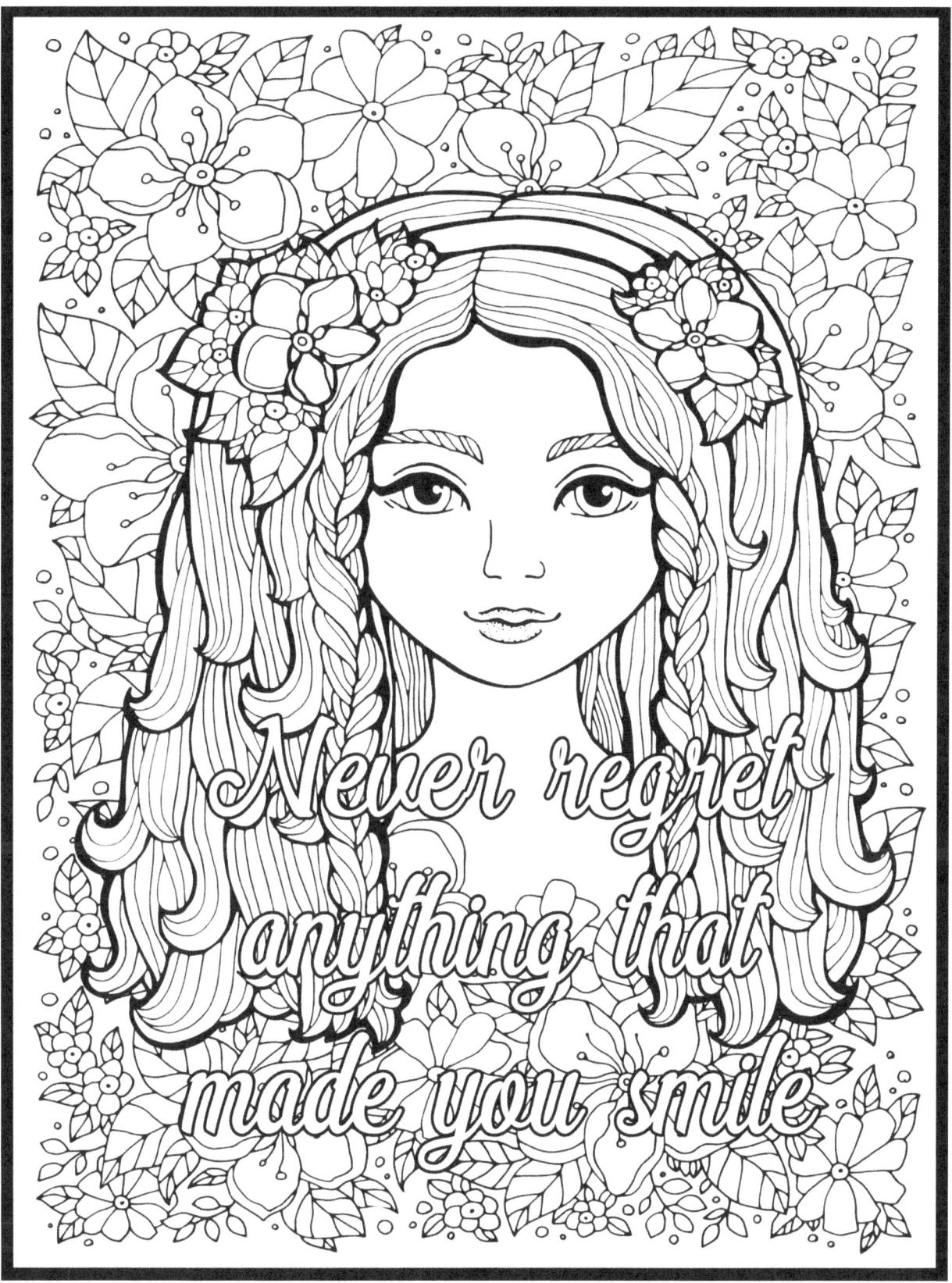

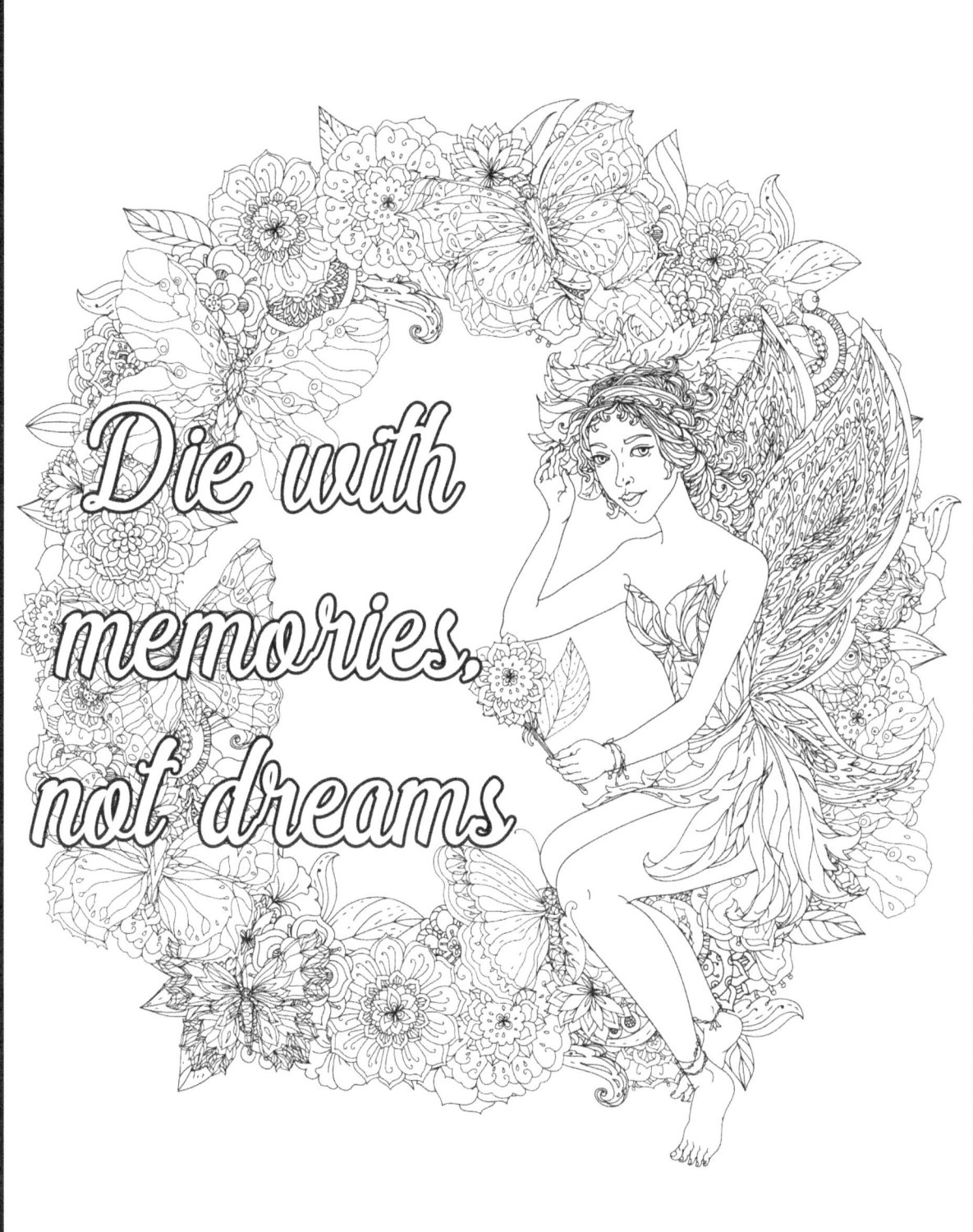

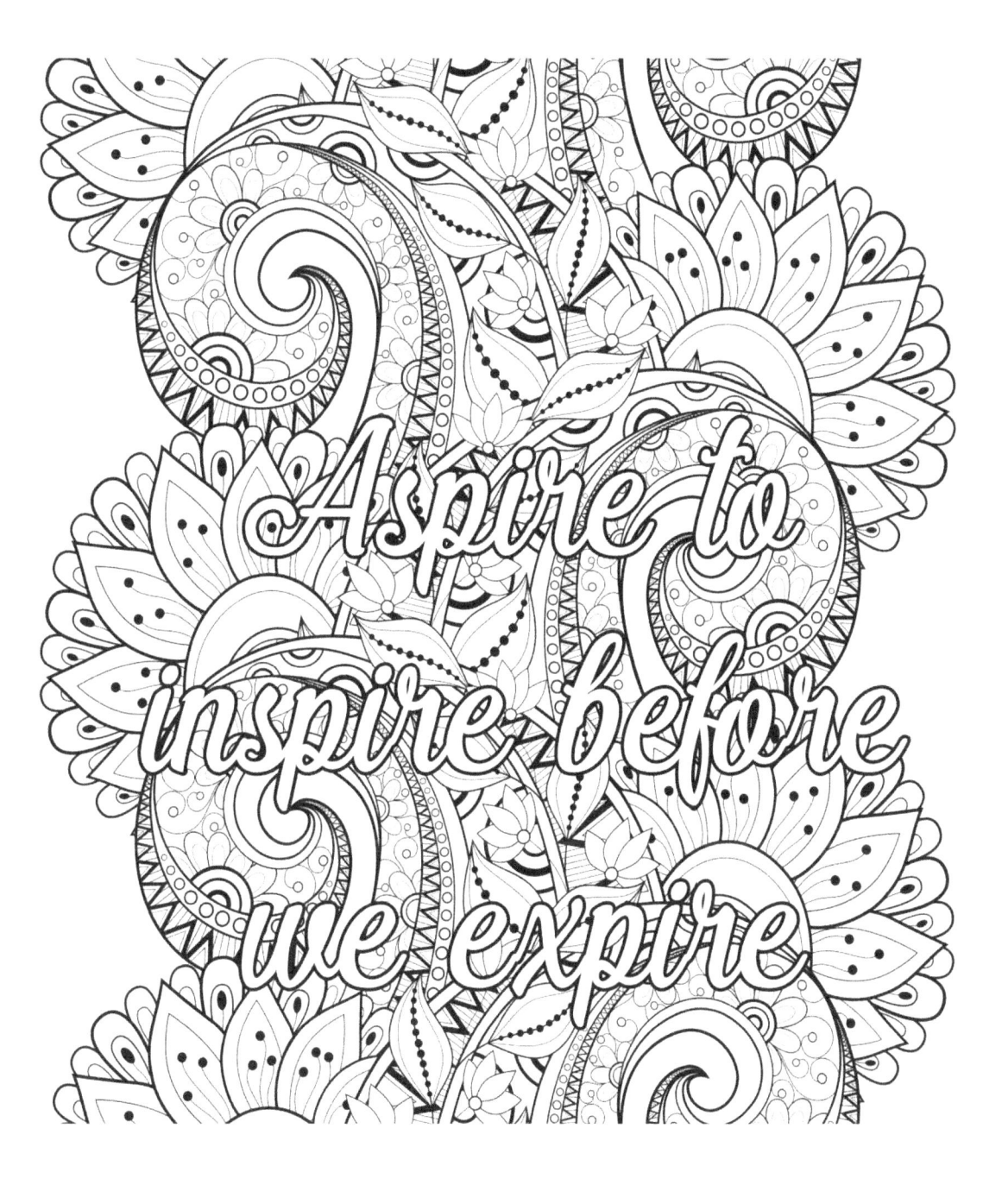

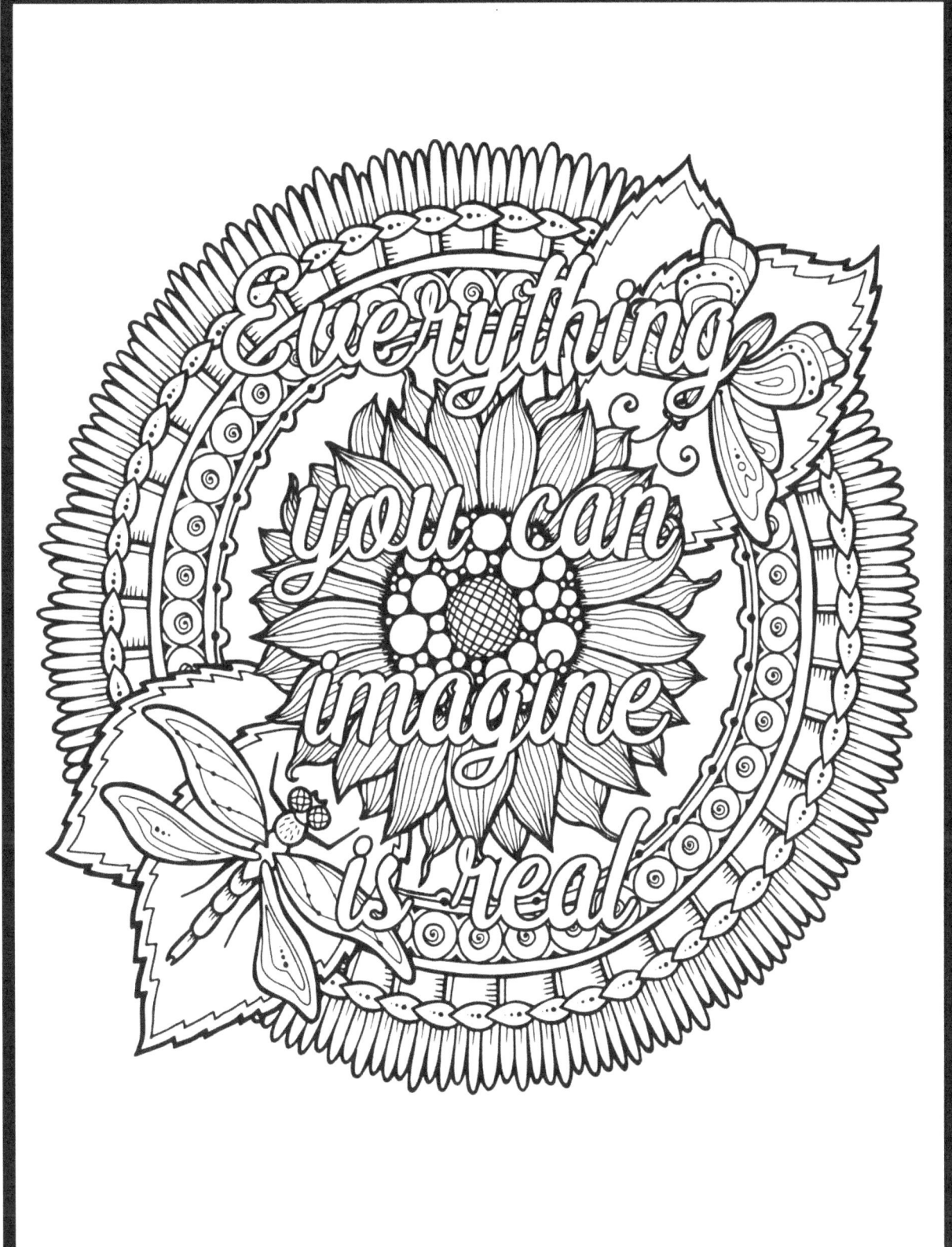

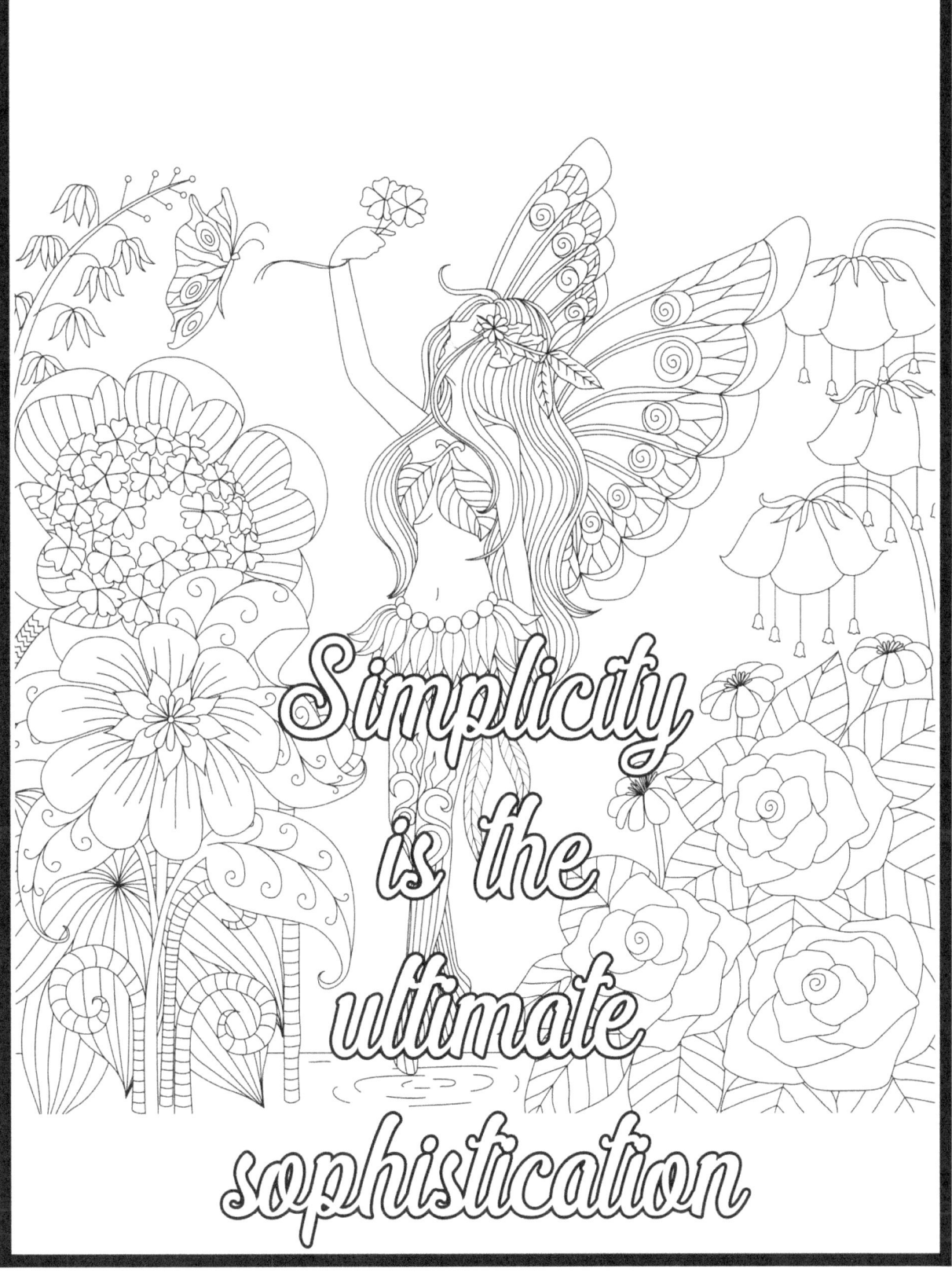

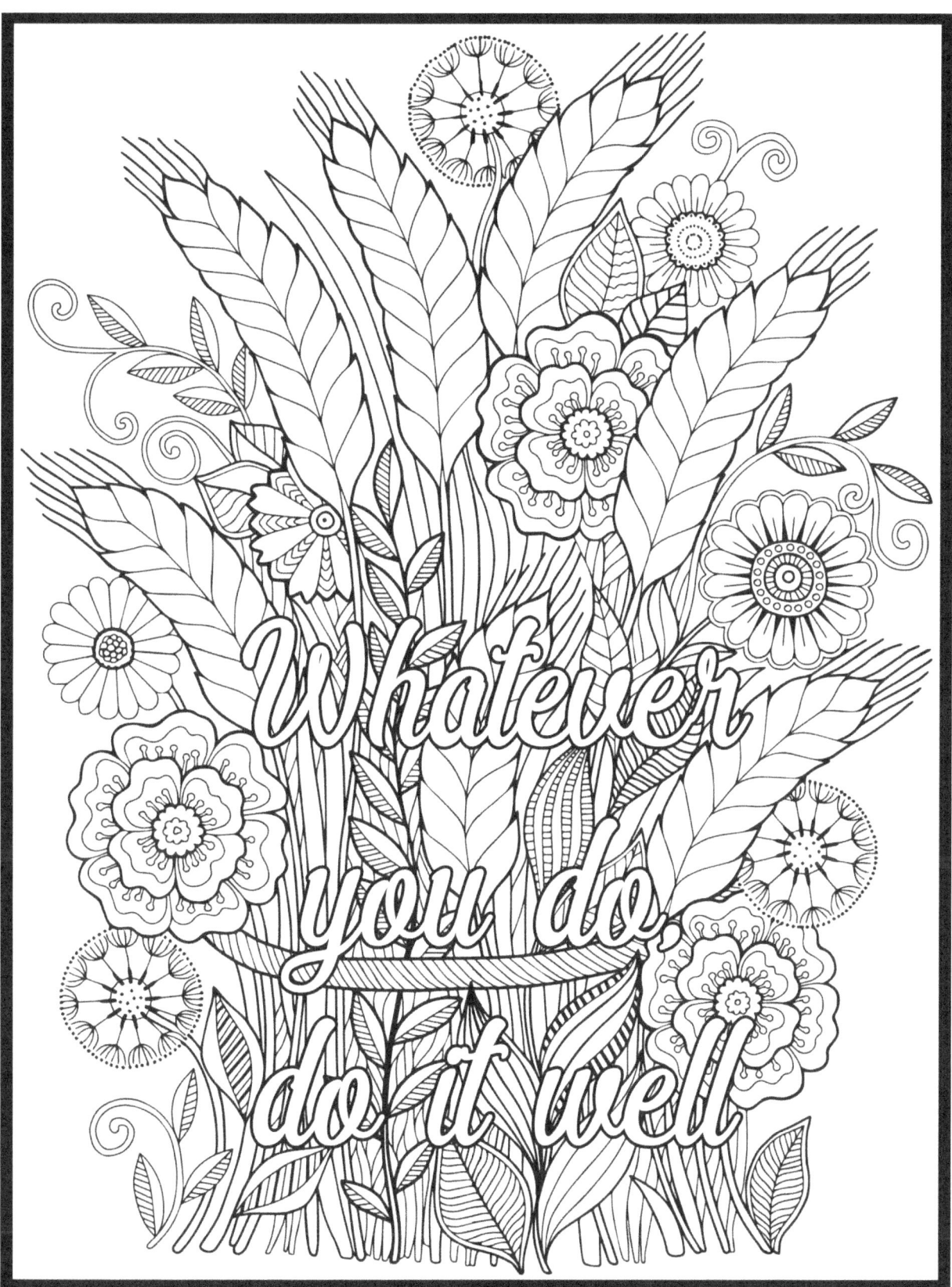

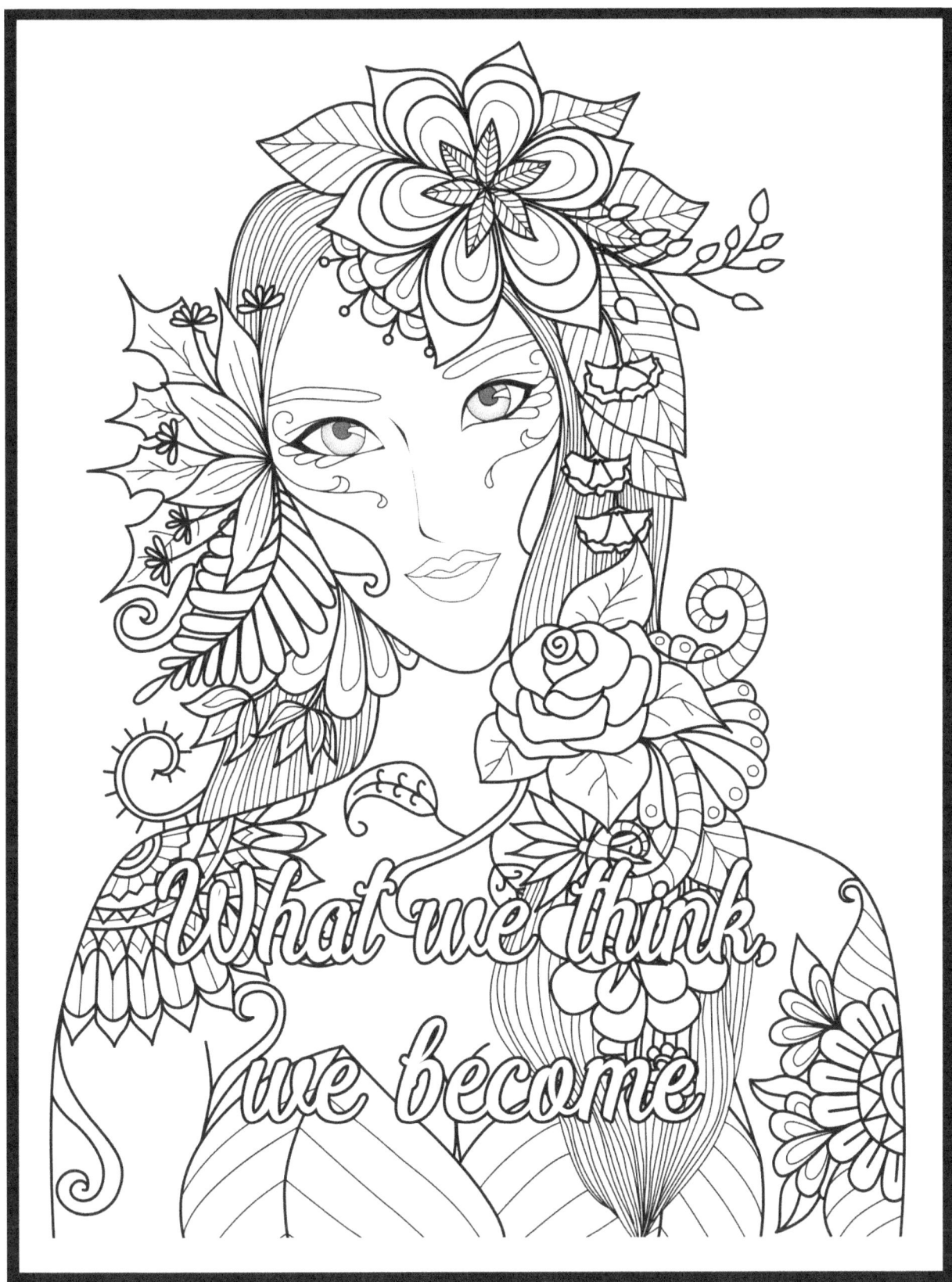

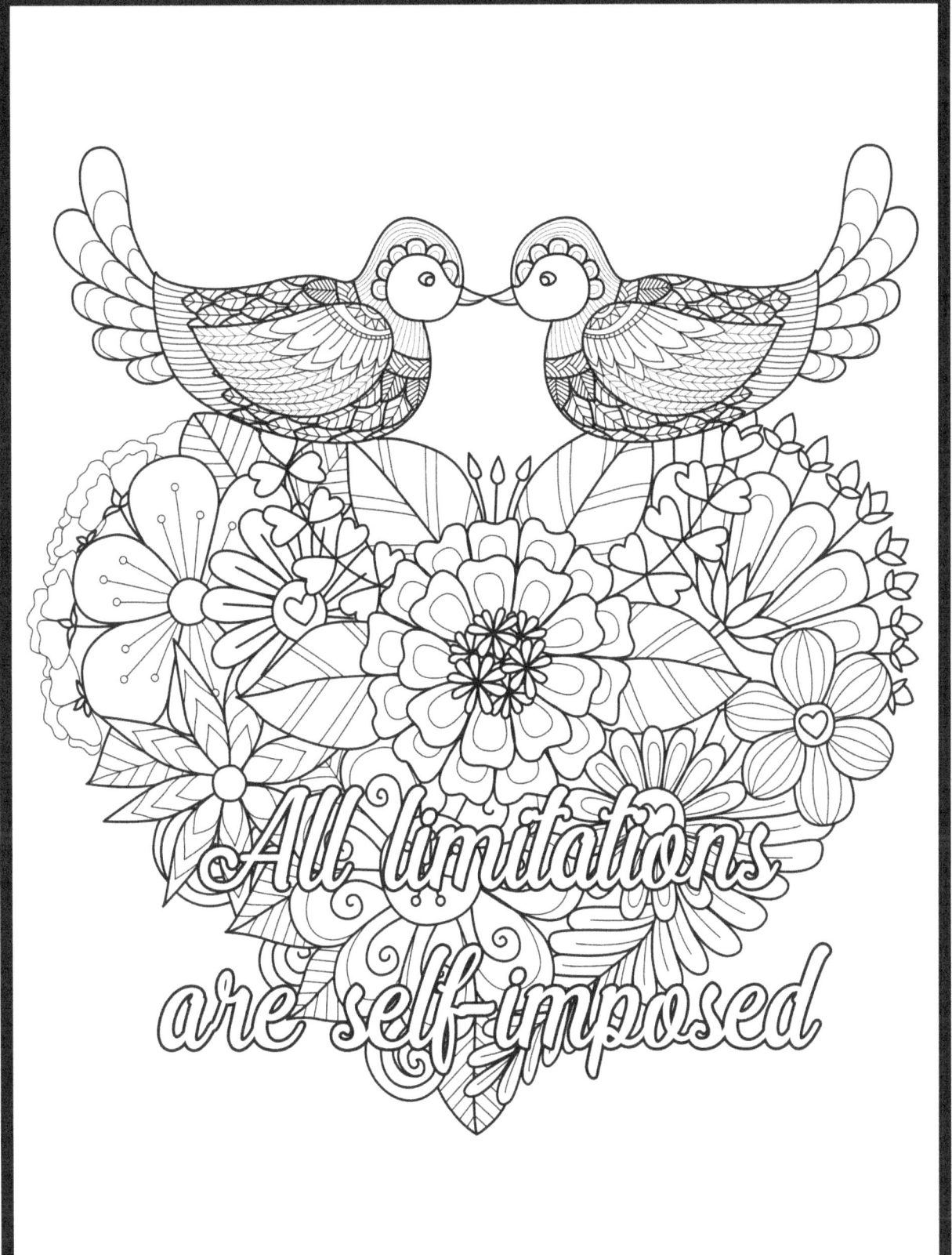

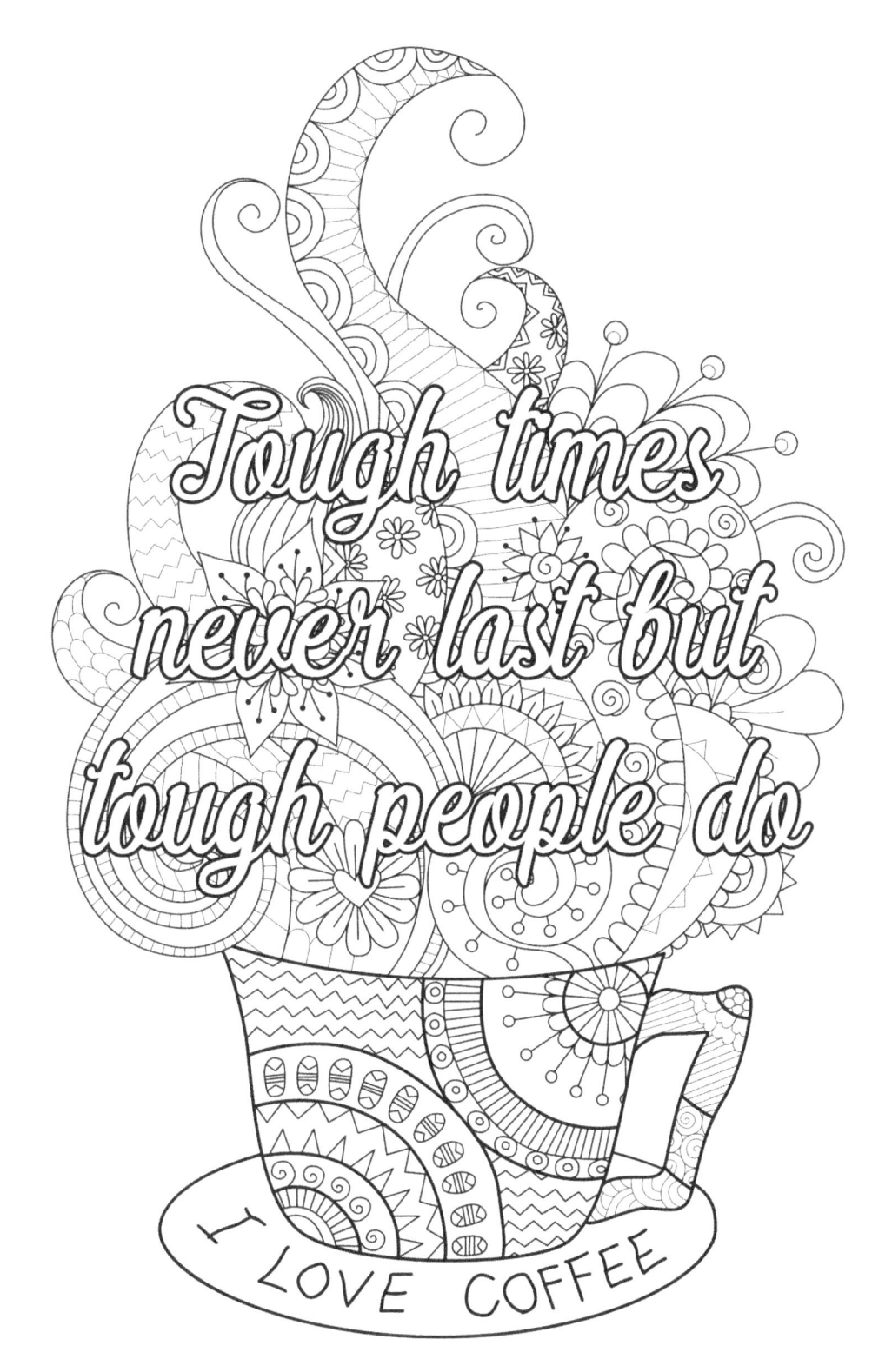

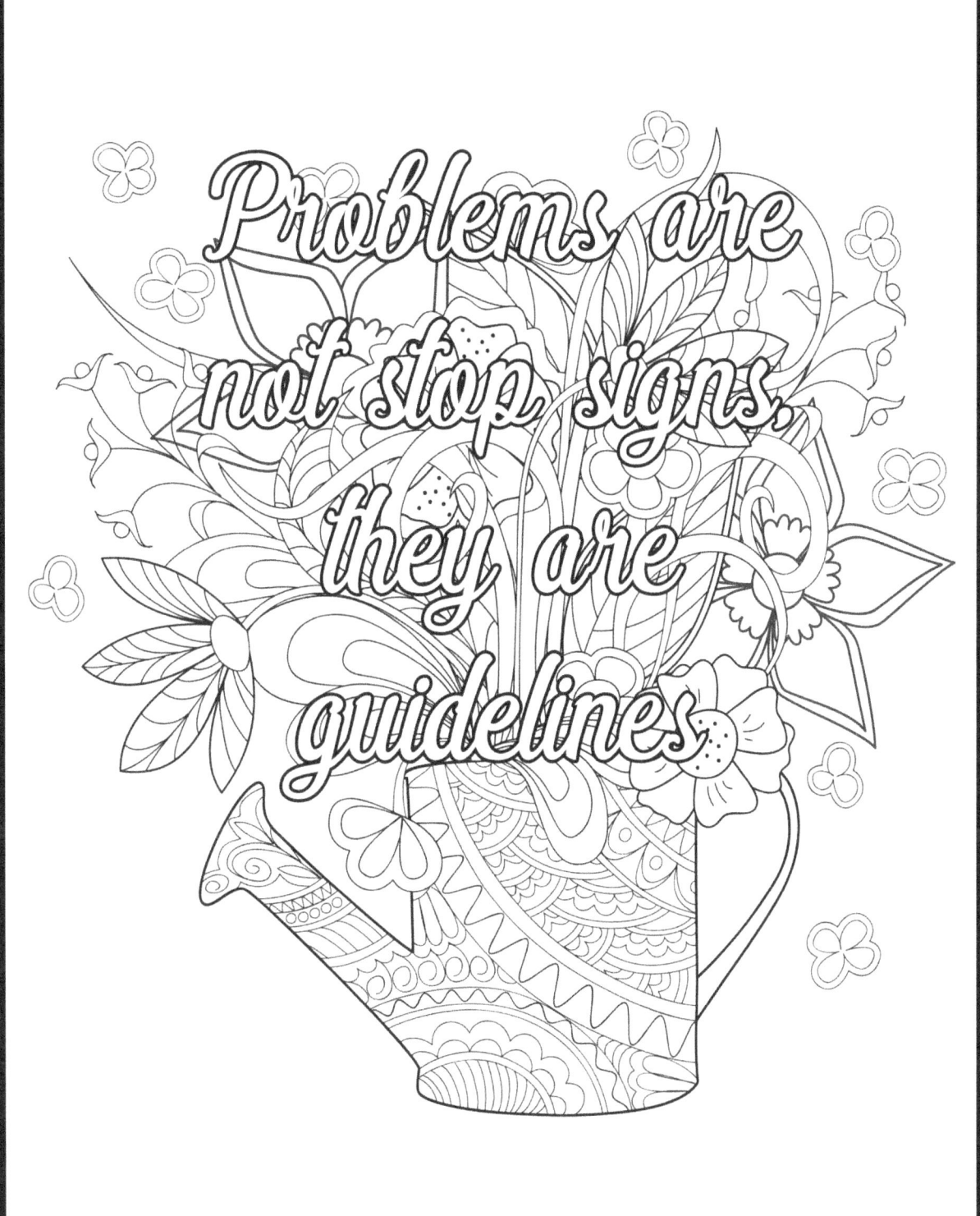

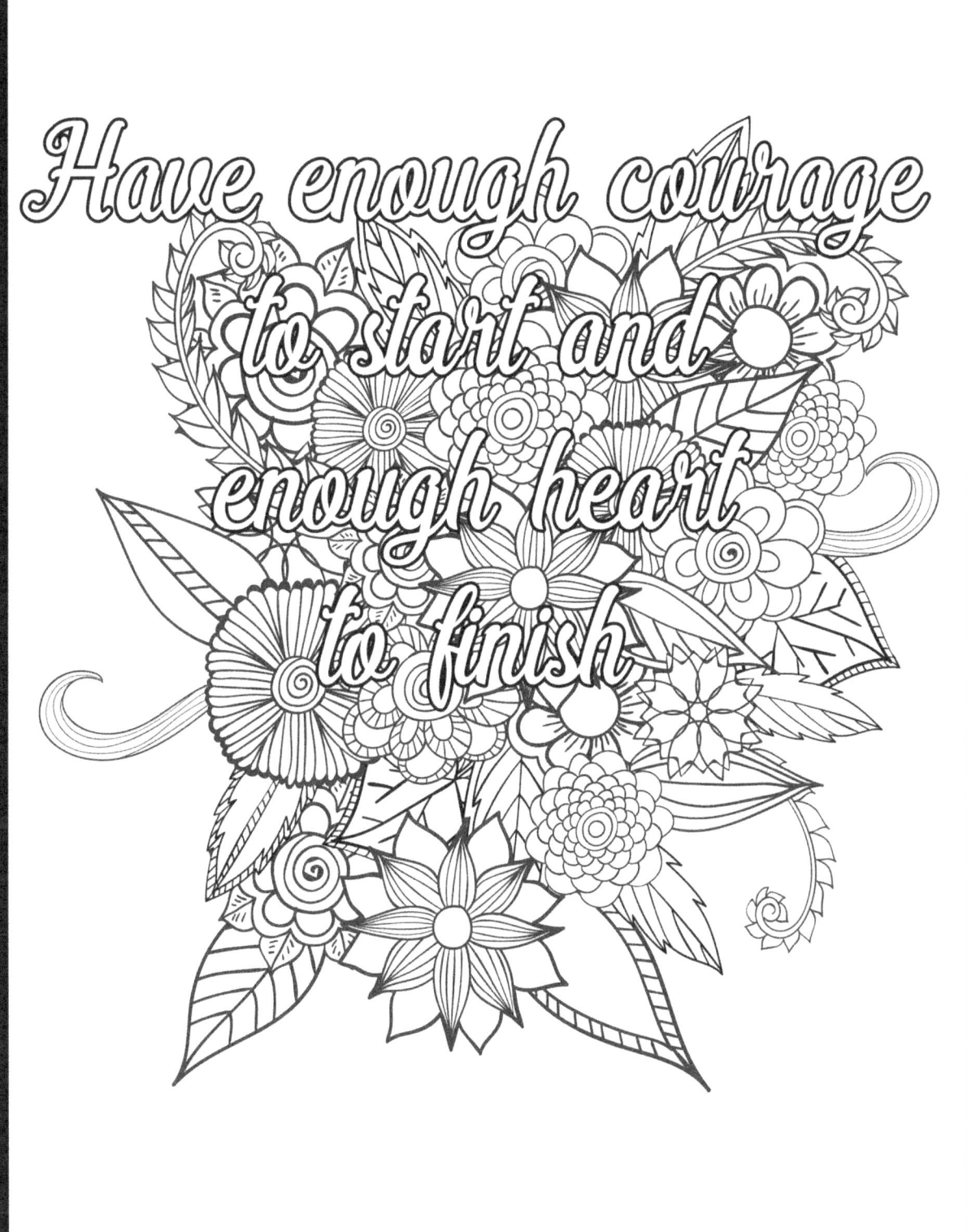

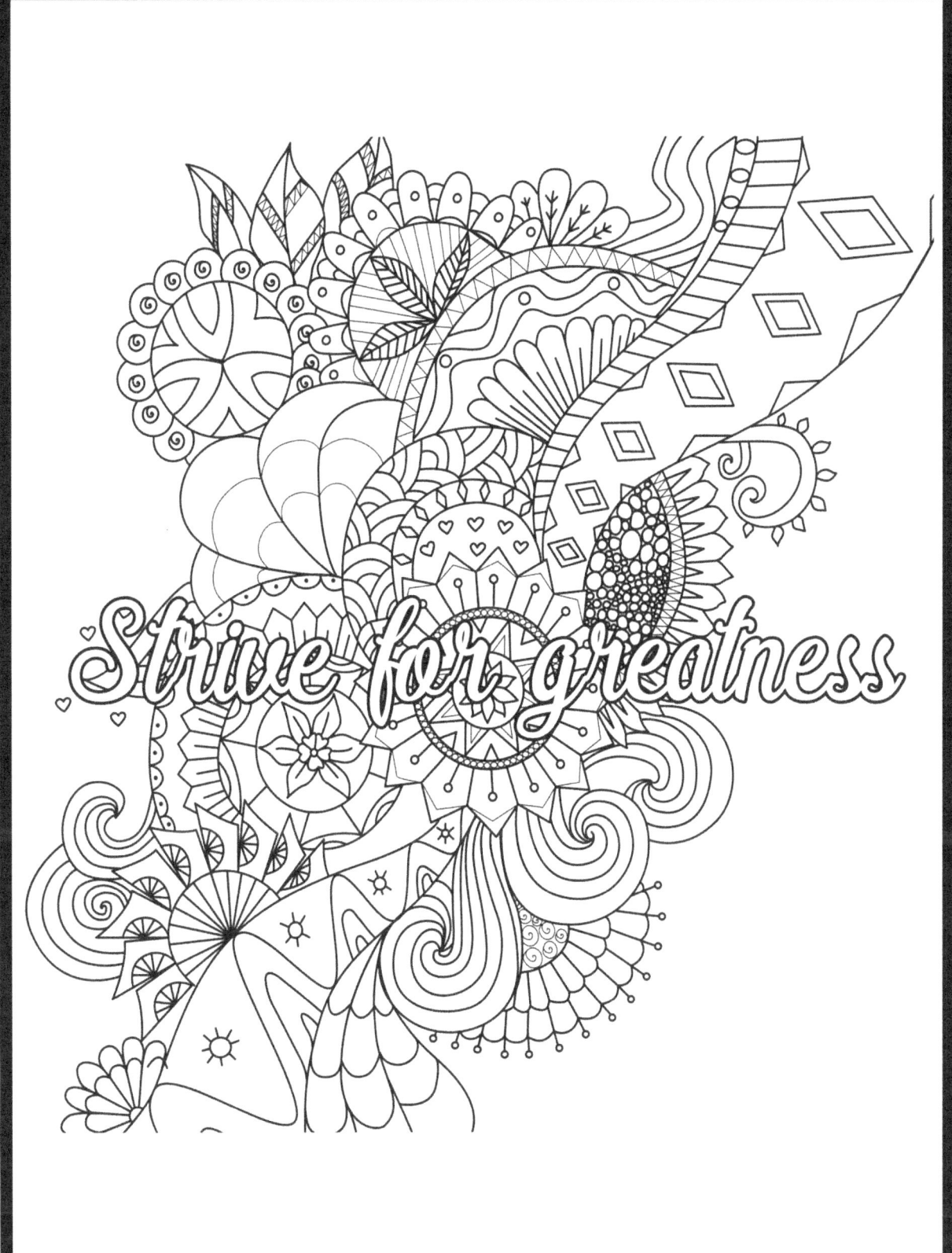

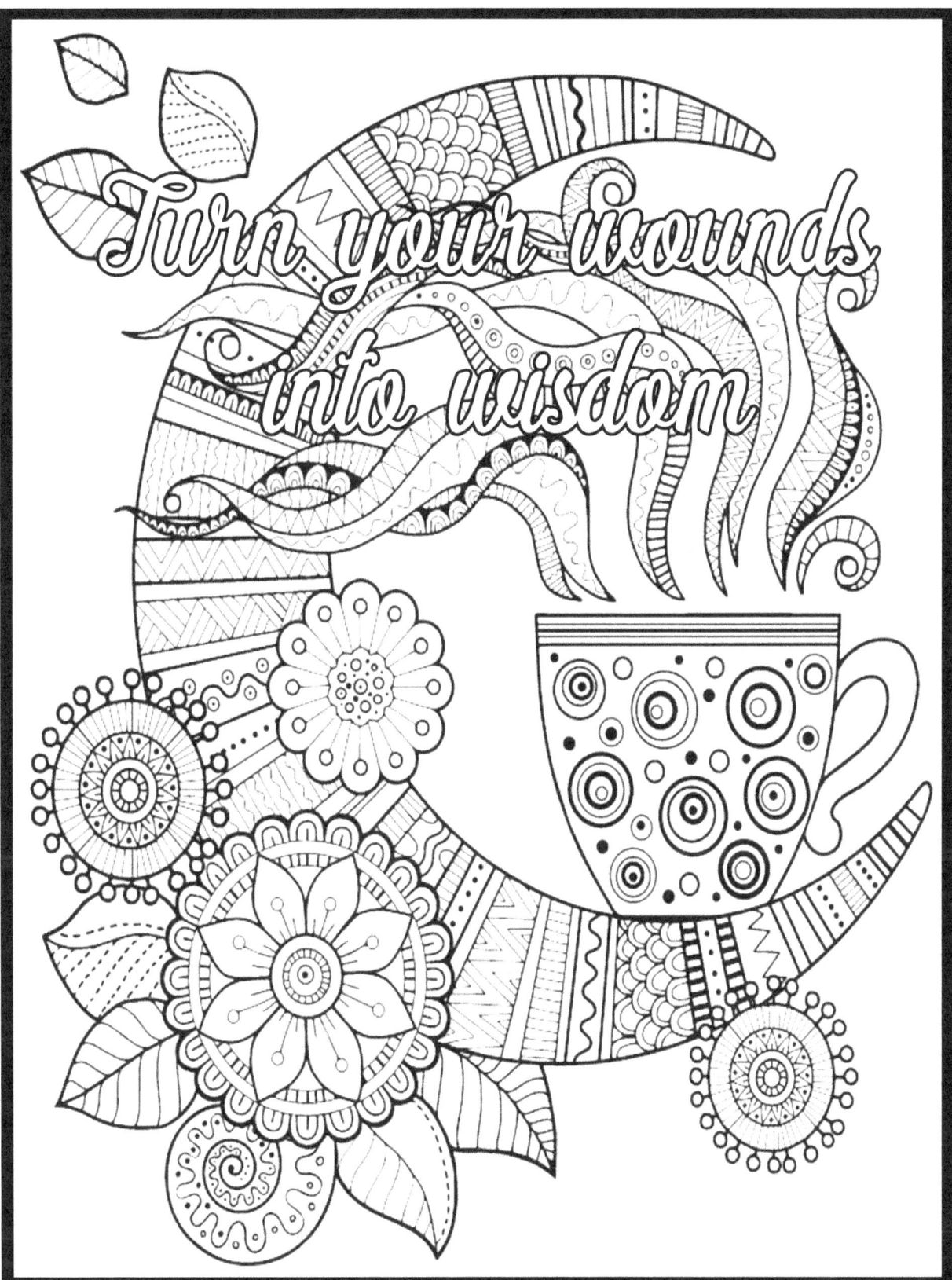

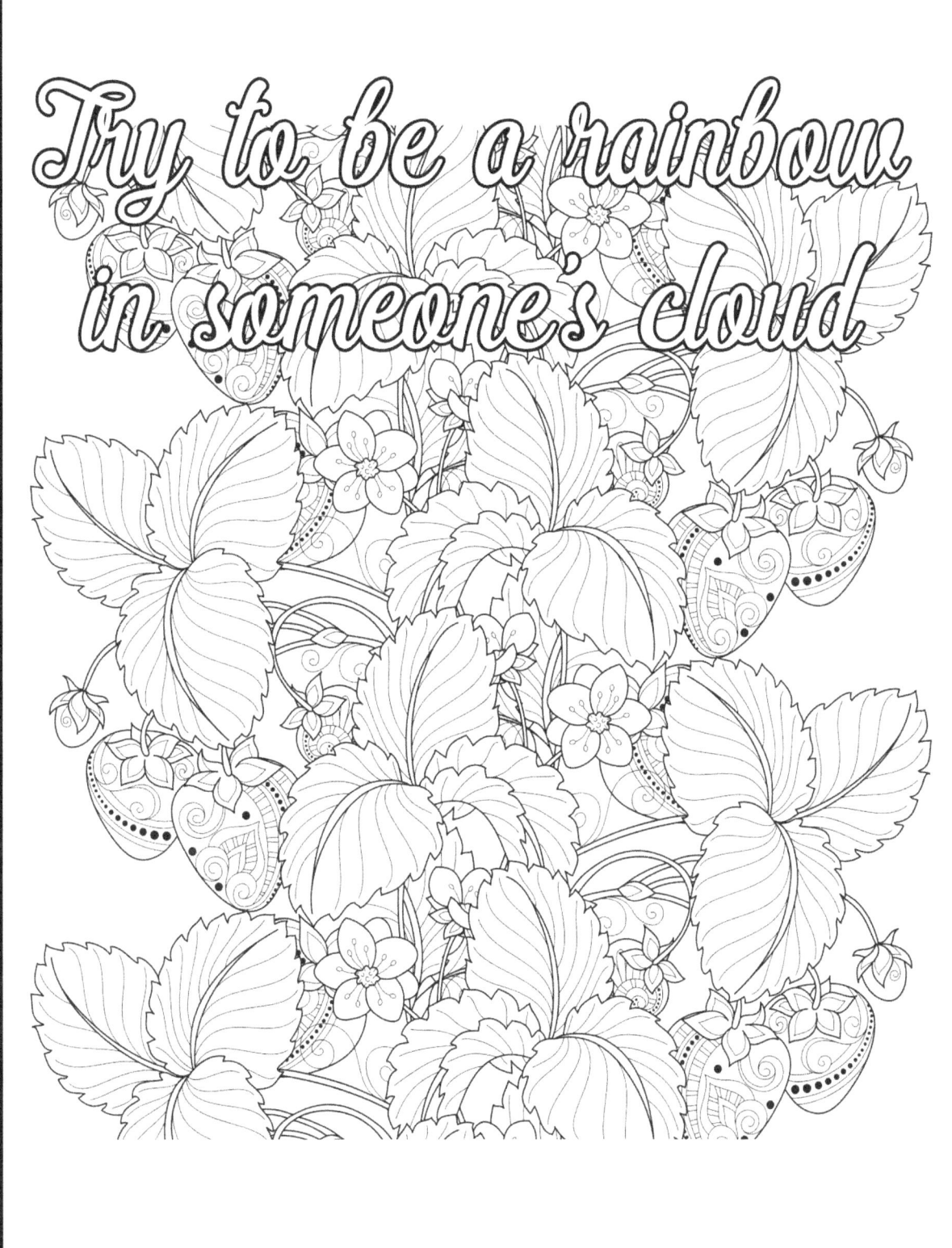

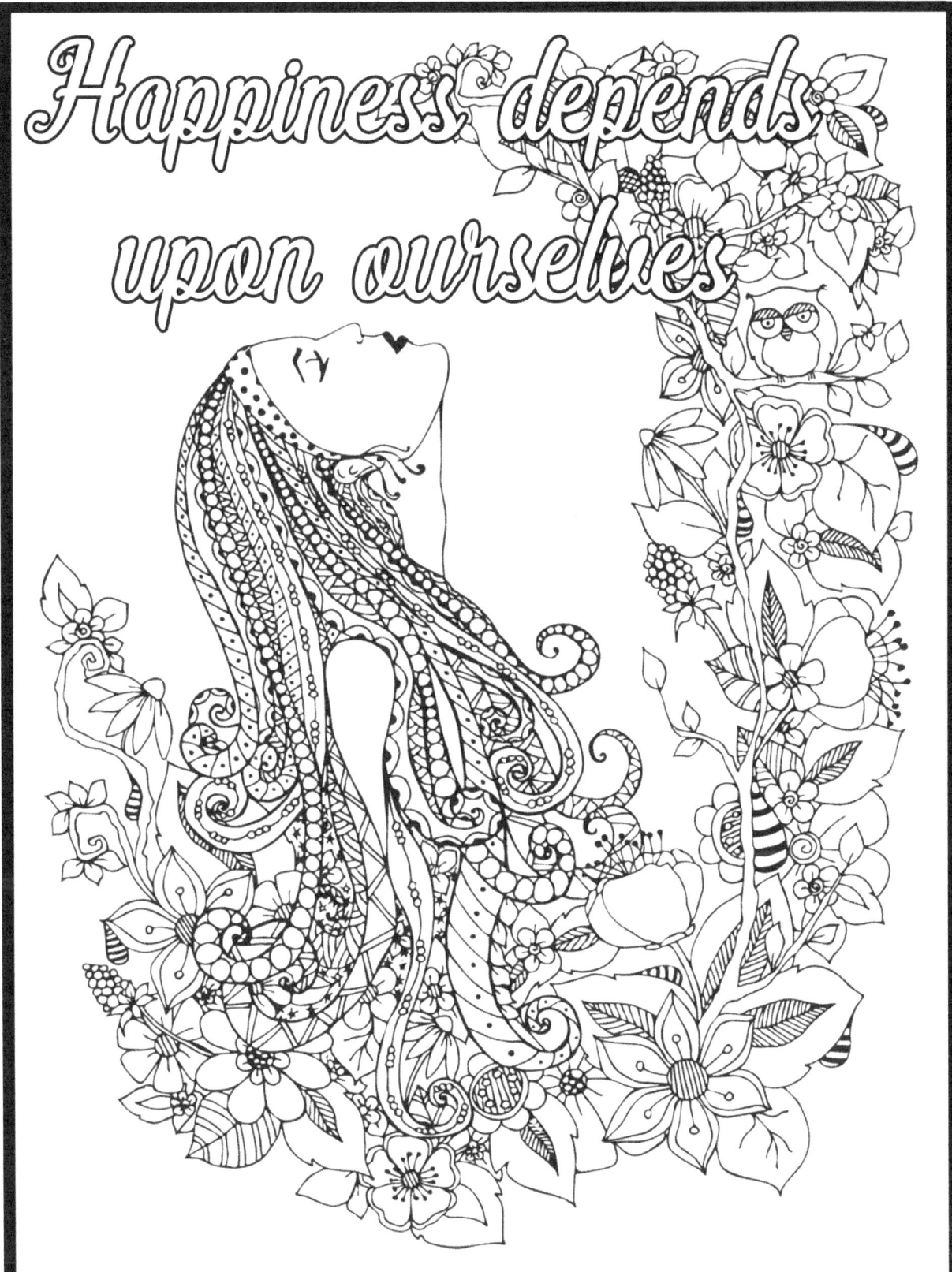

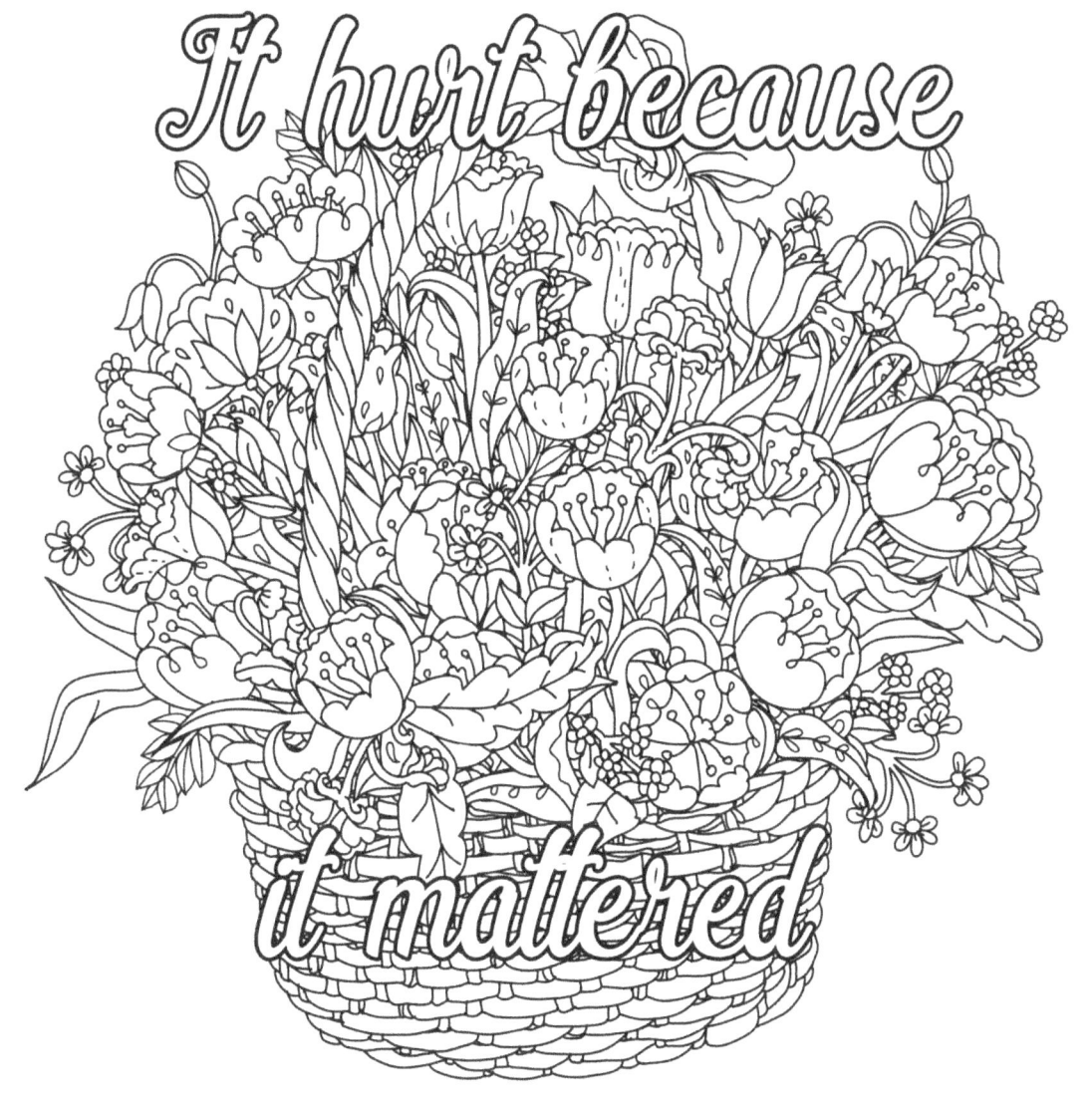

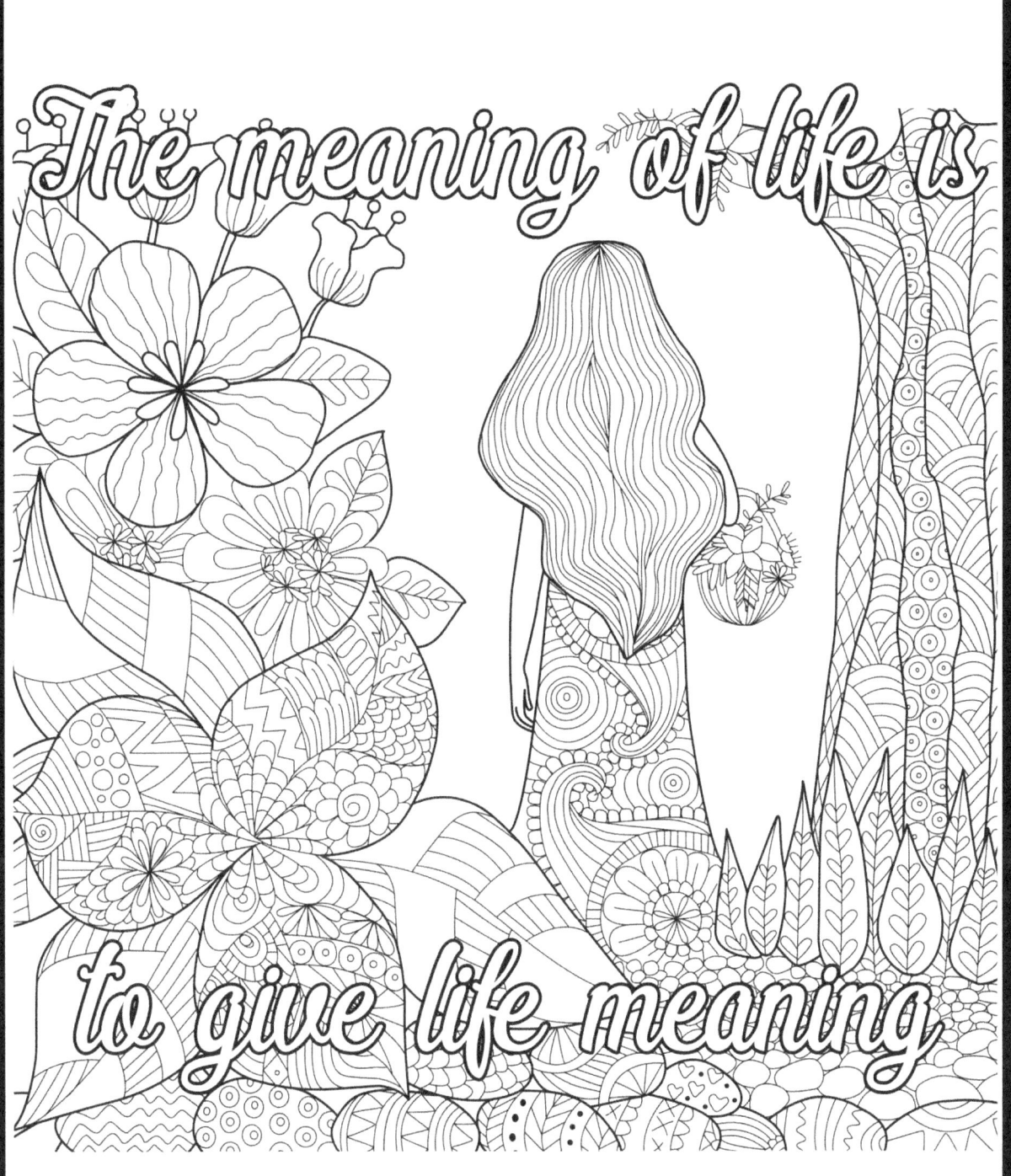

Be yourself, everyone else is already taken

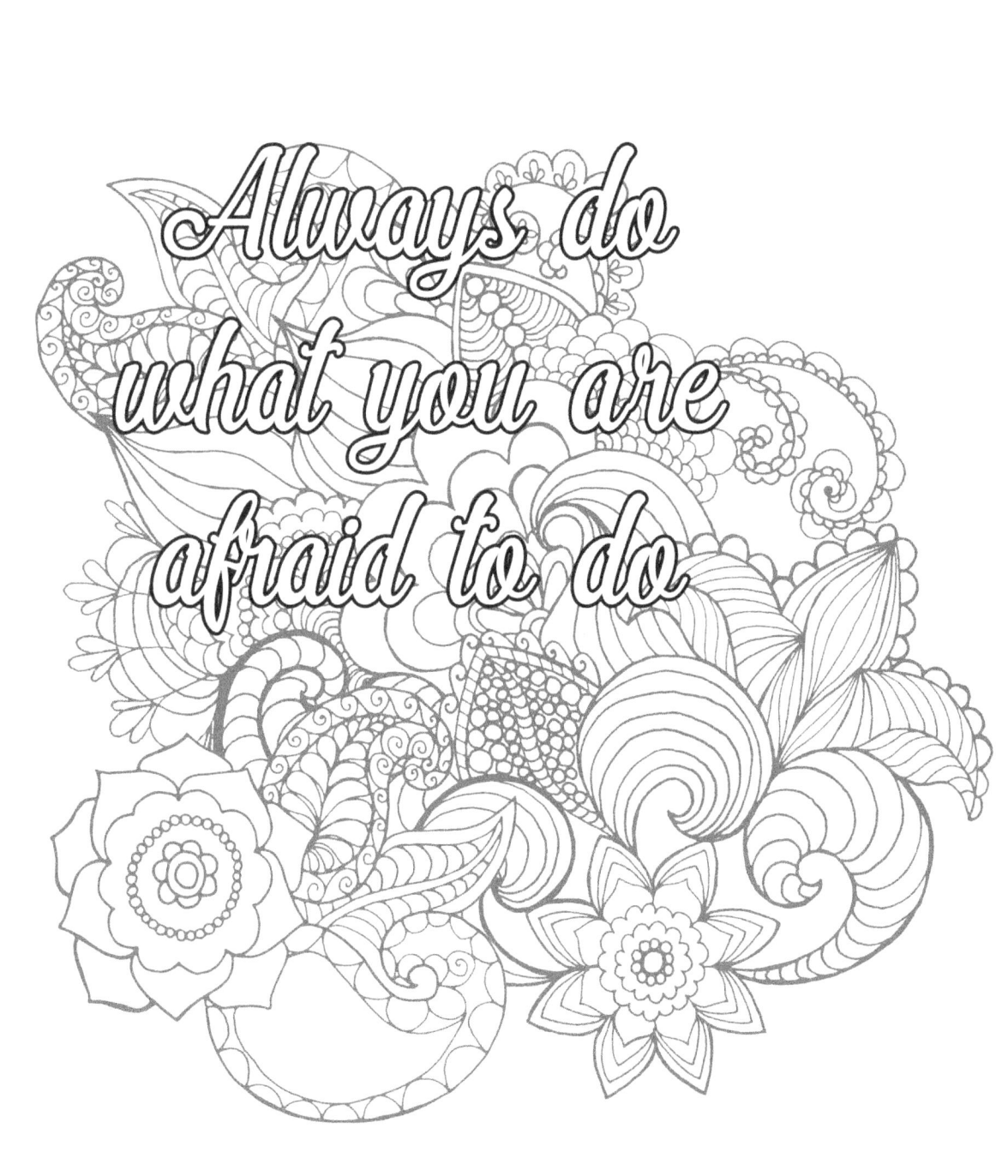

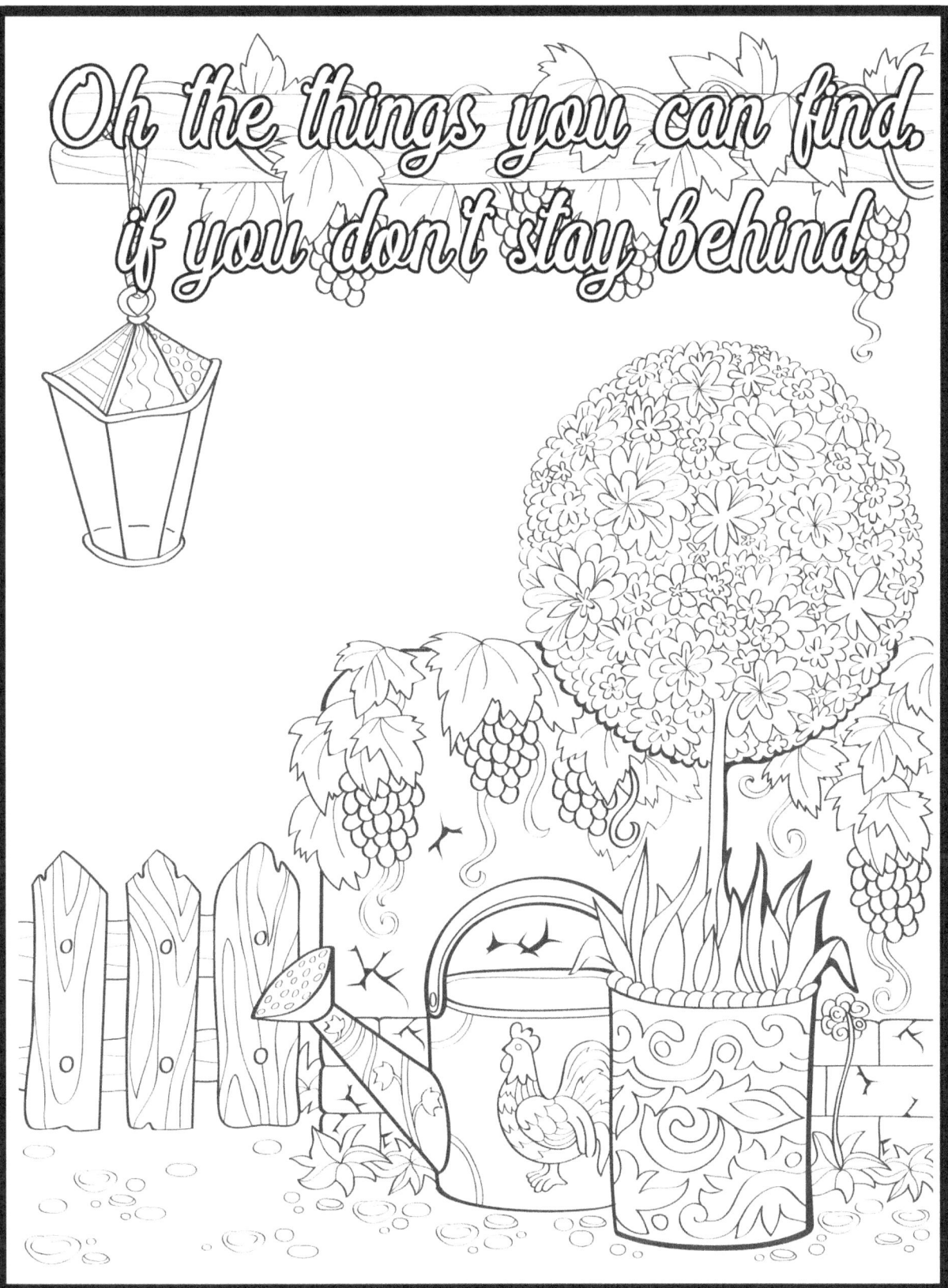

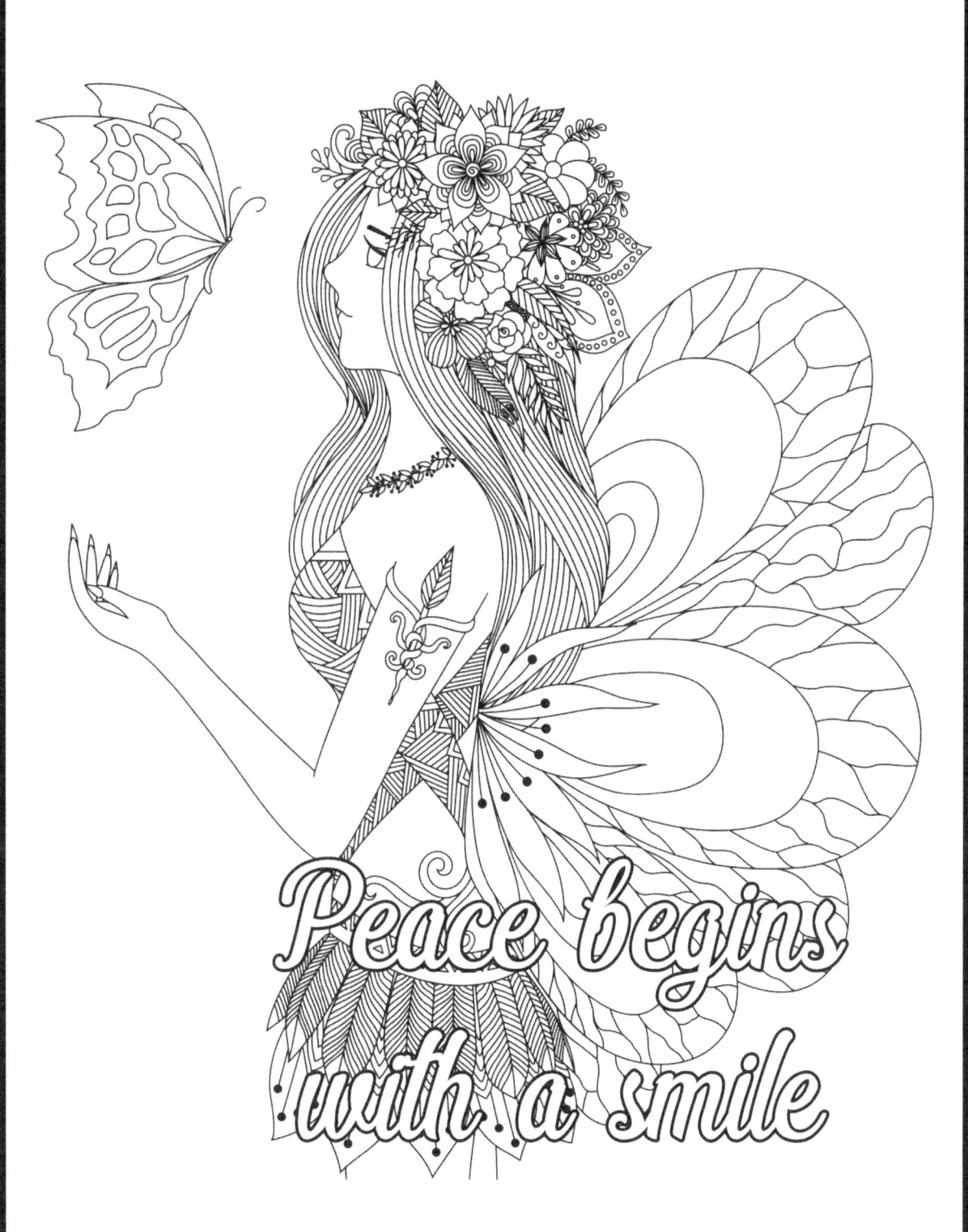

When words fail, music speaks

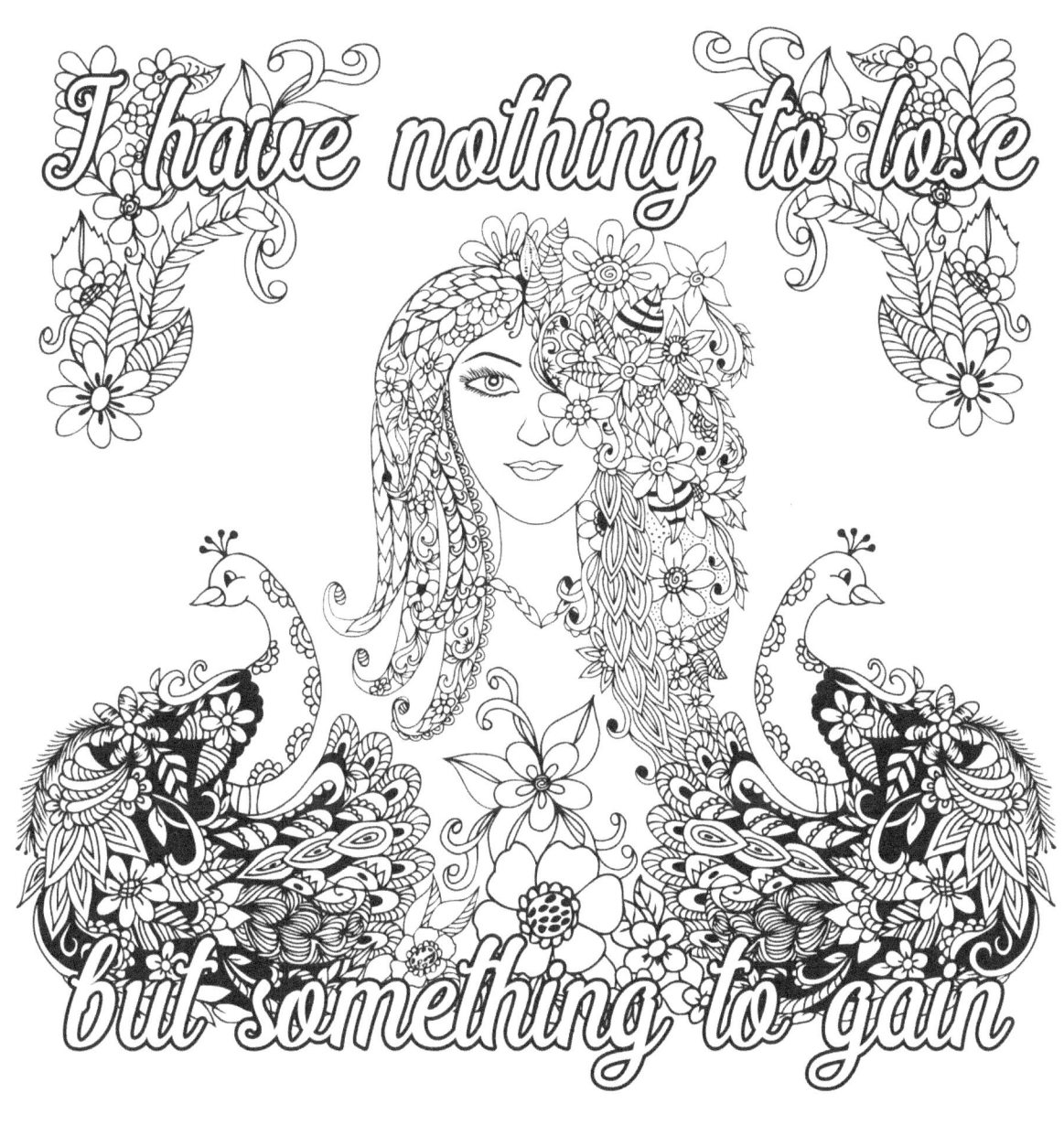

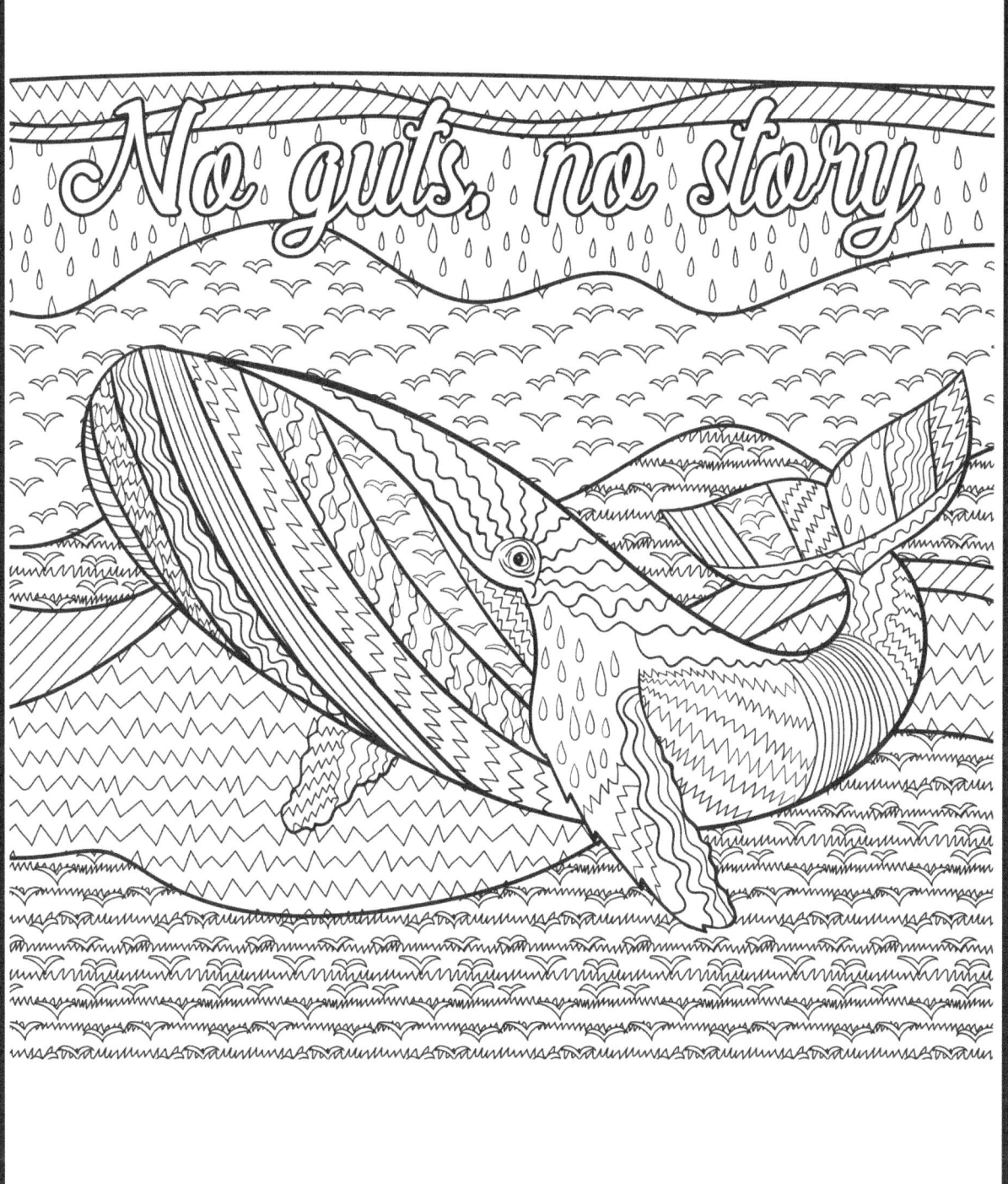

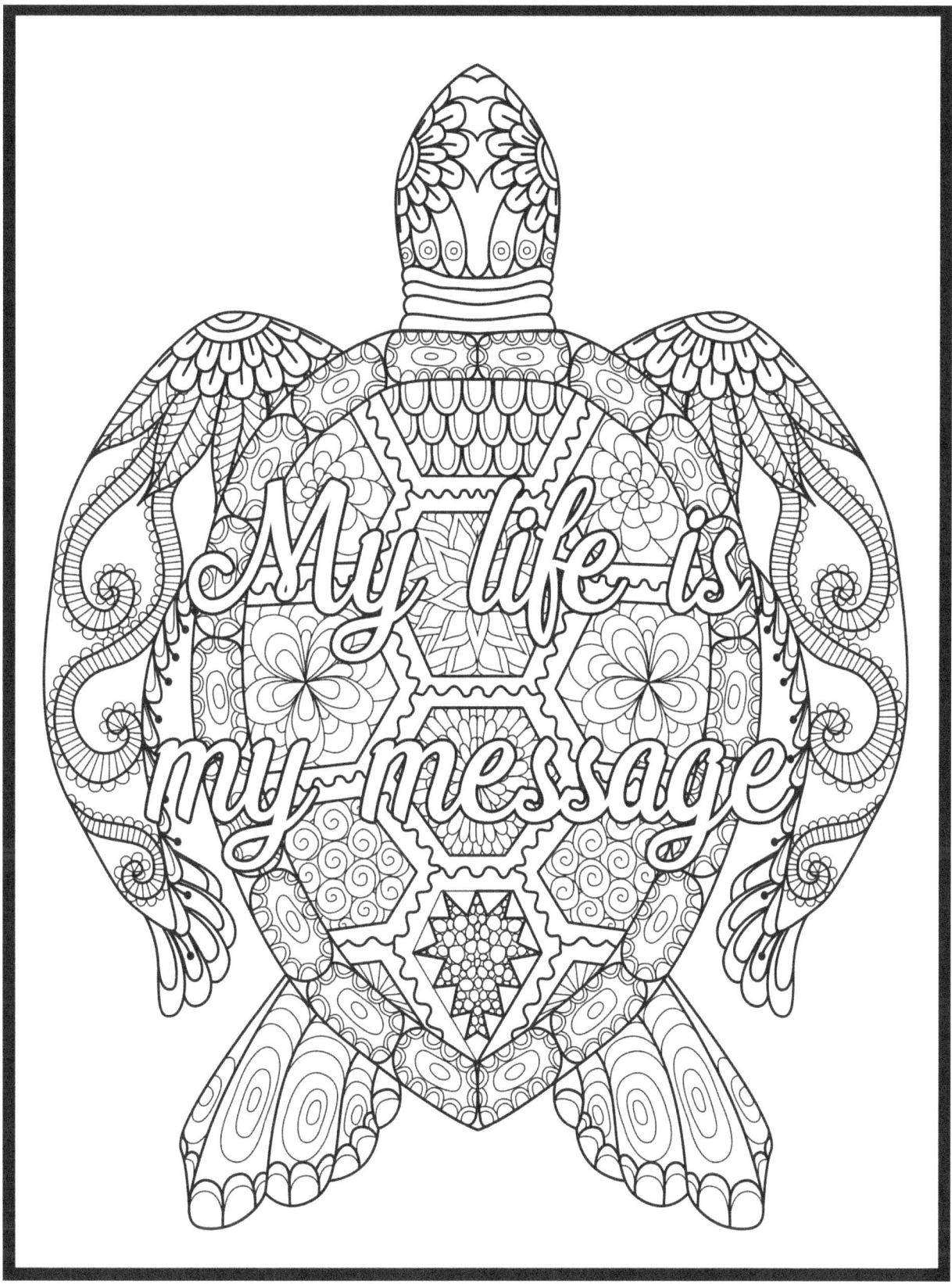

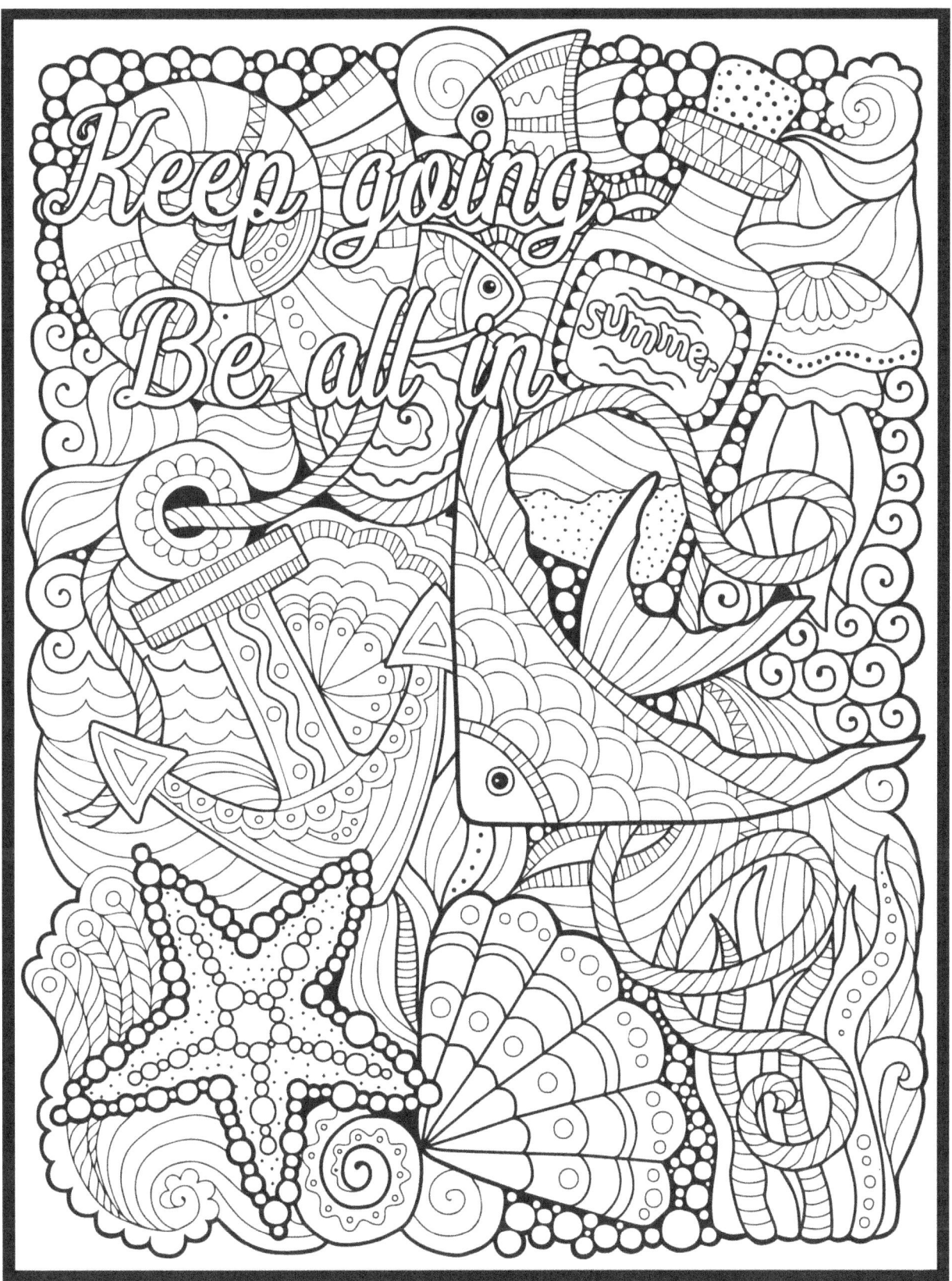

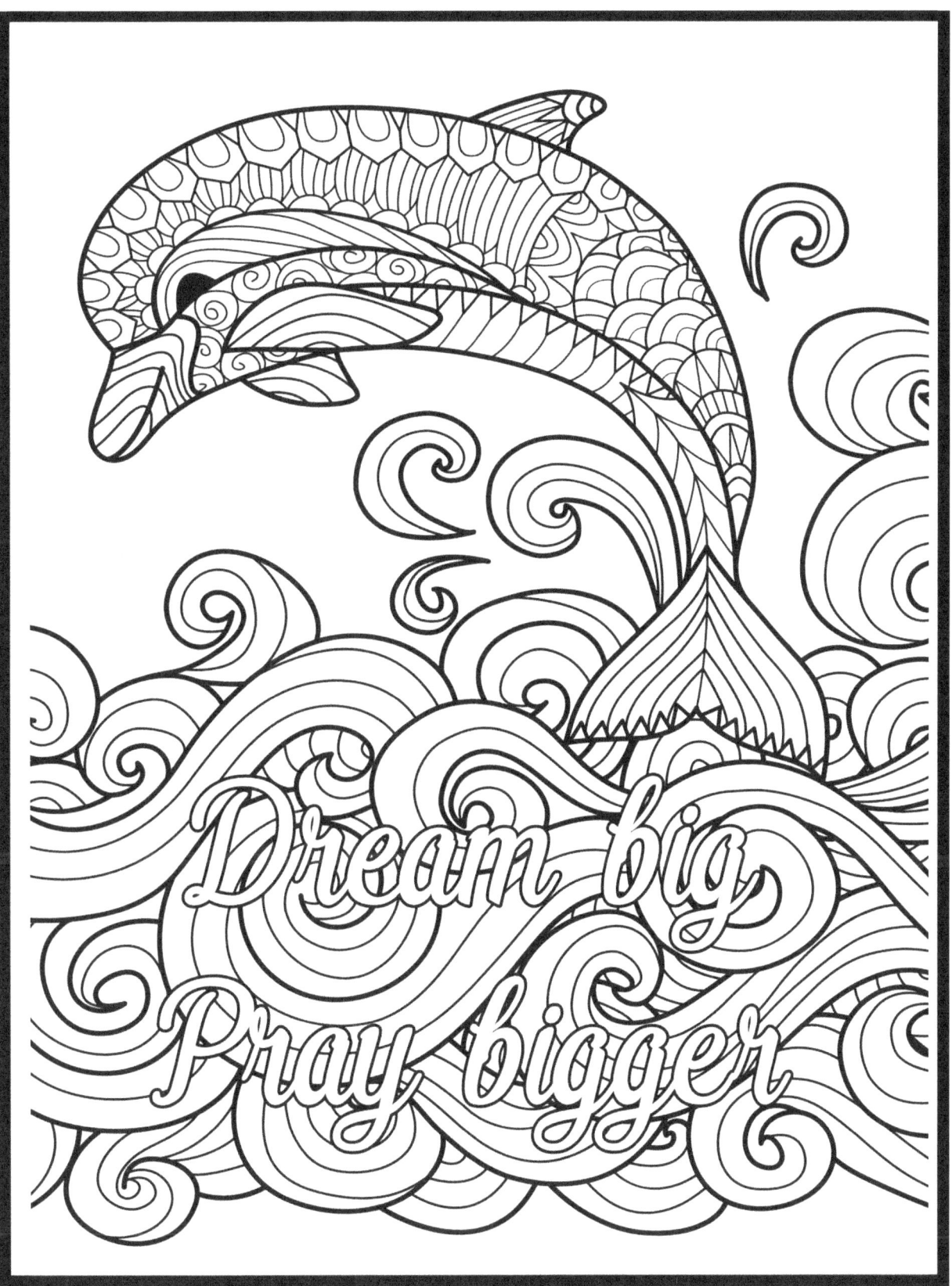

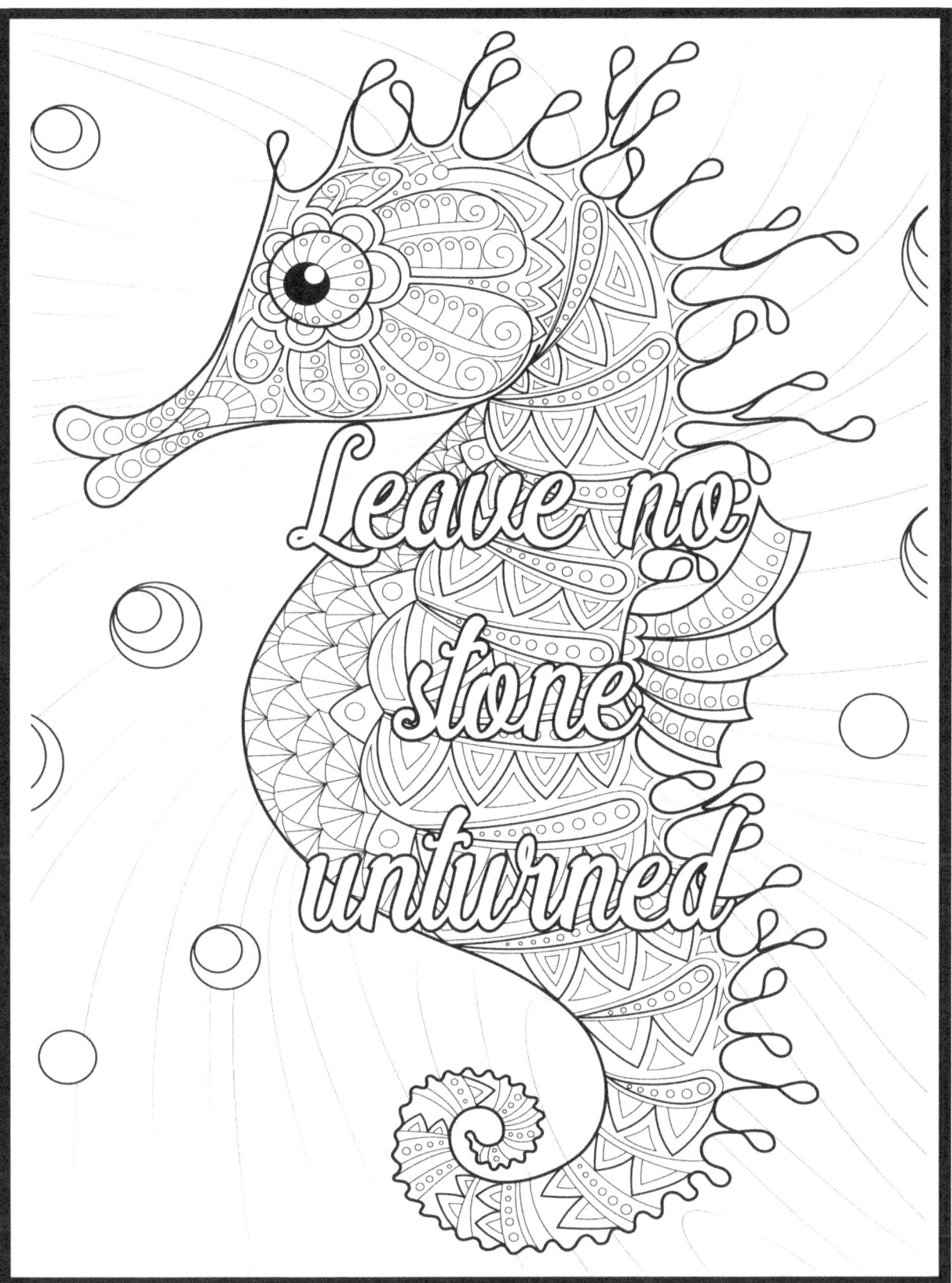

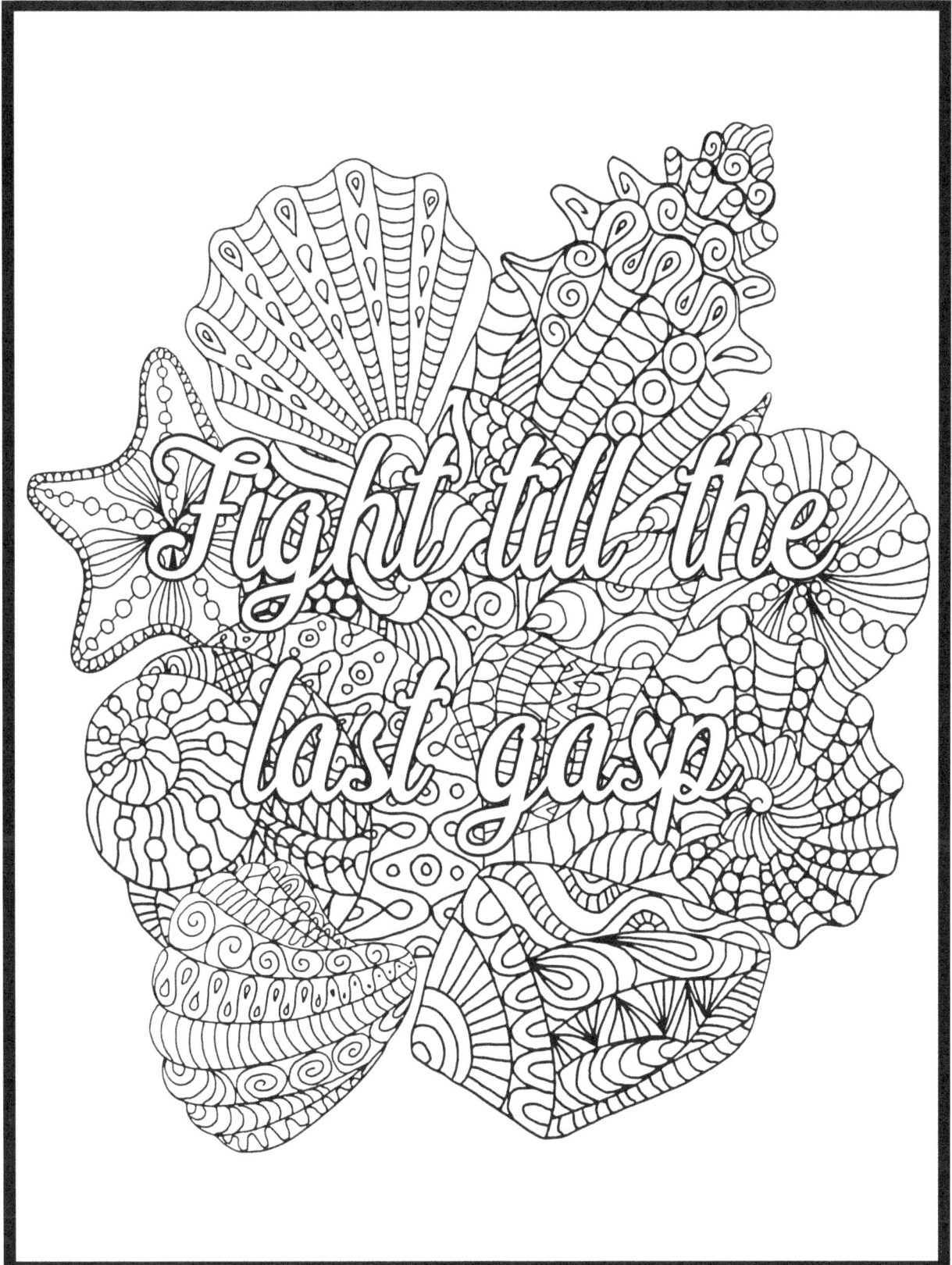

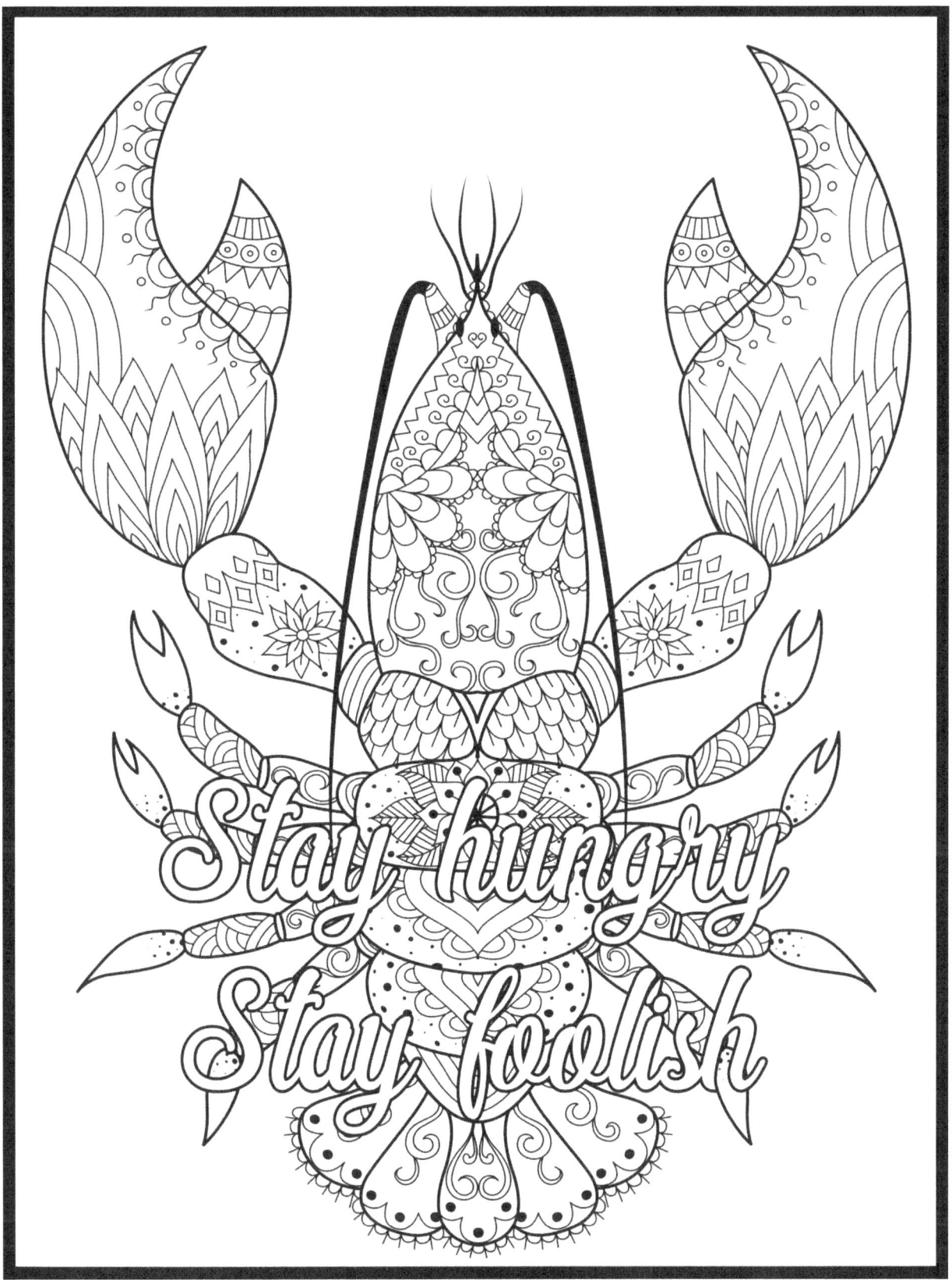

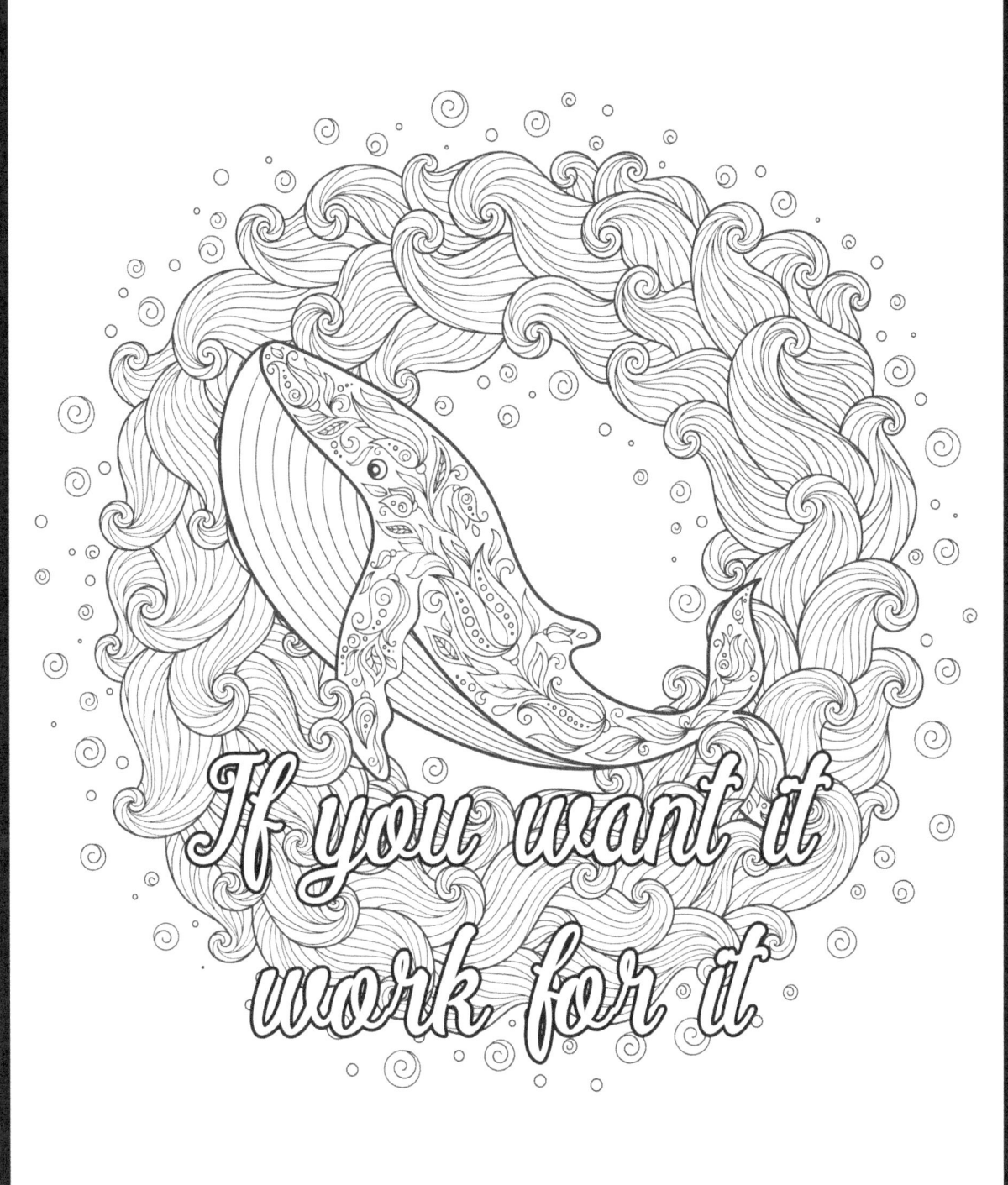

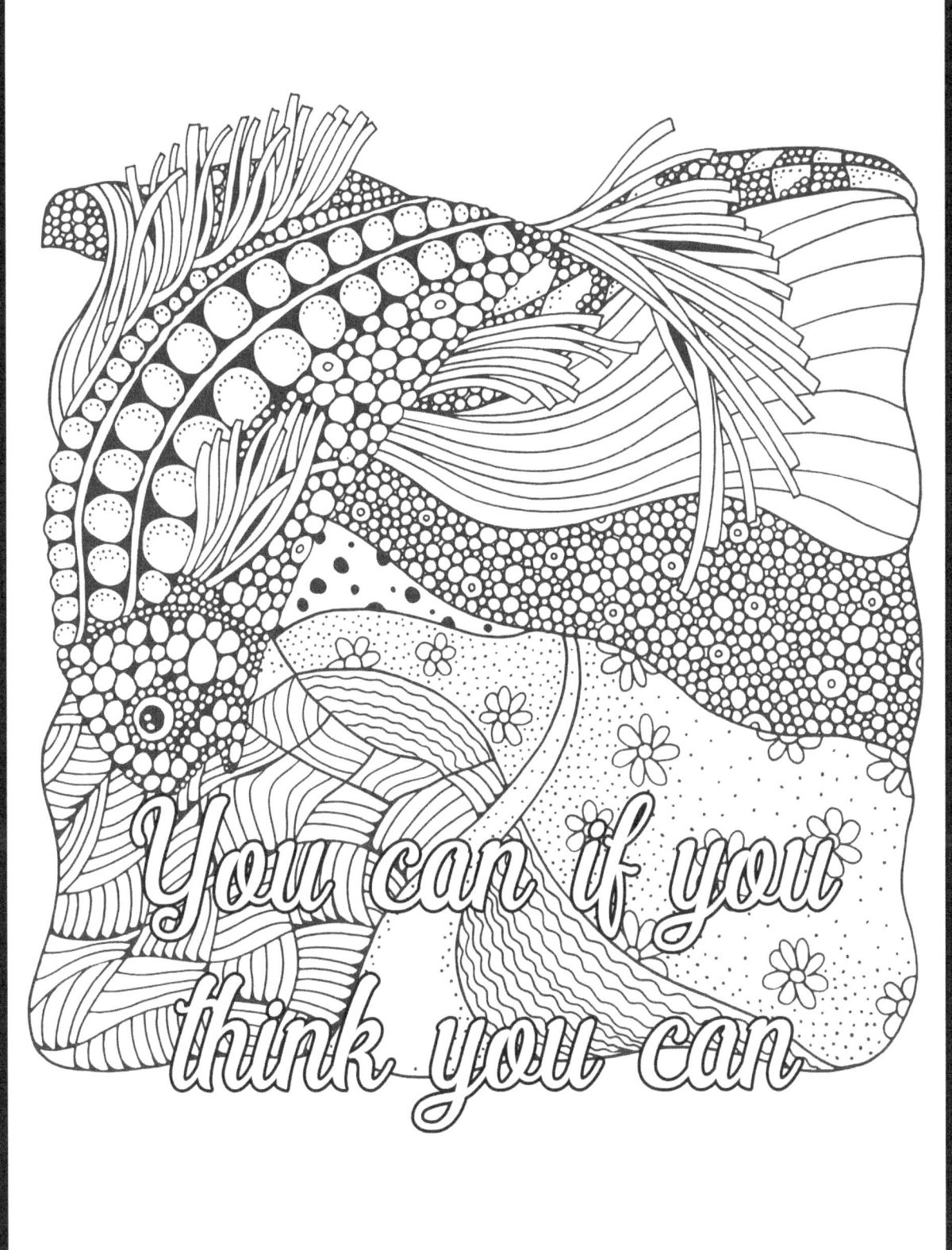

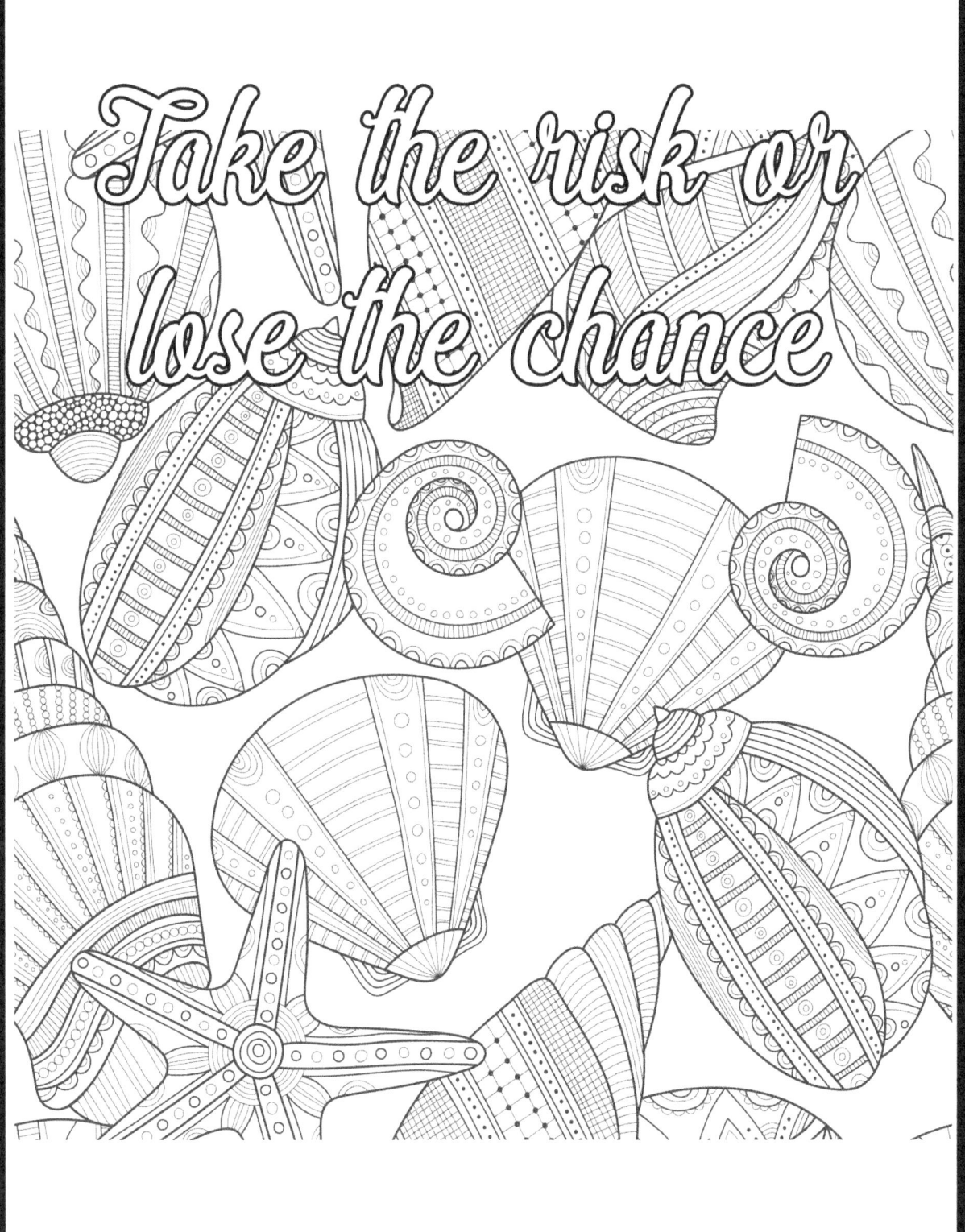

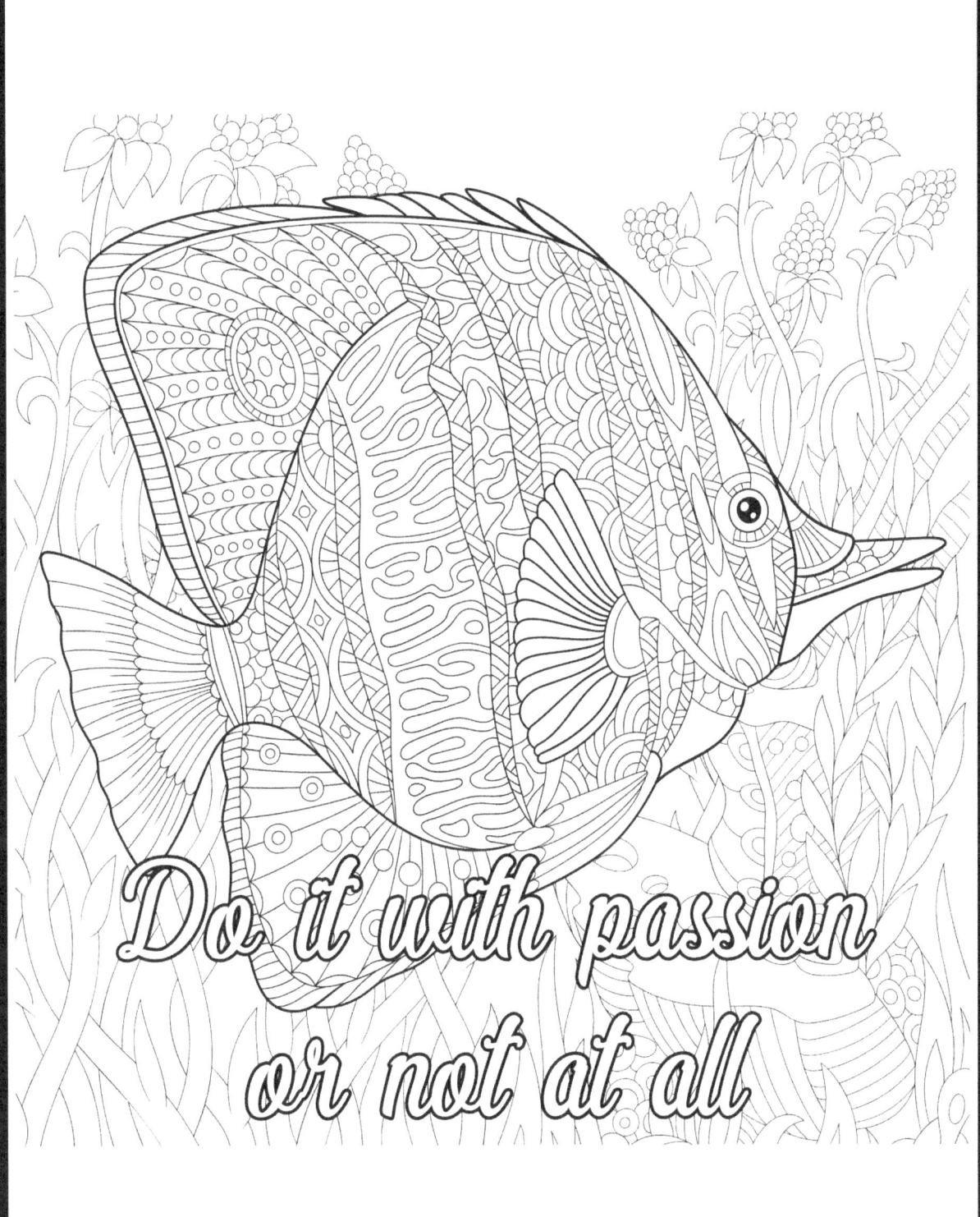

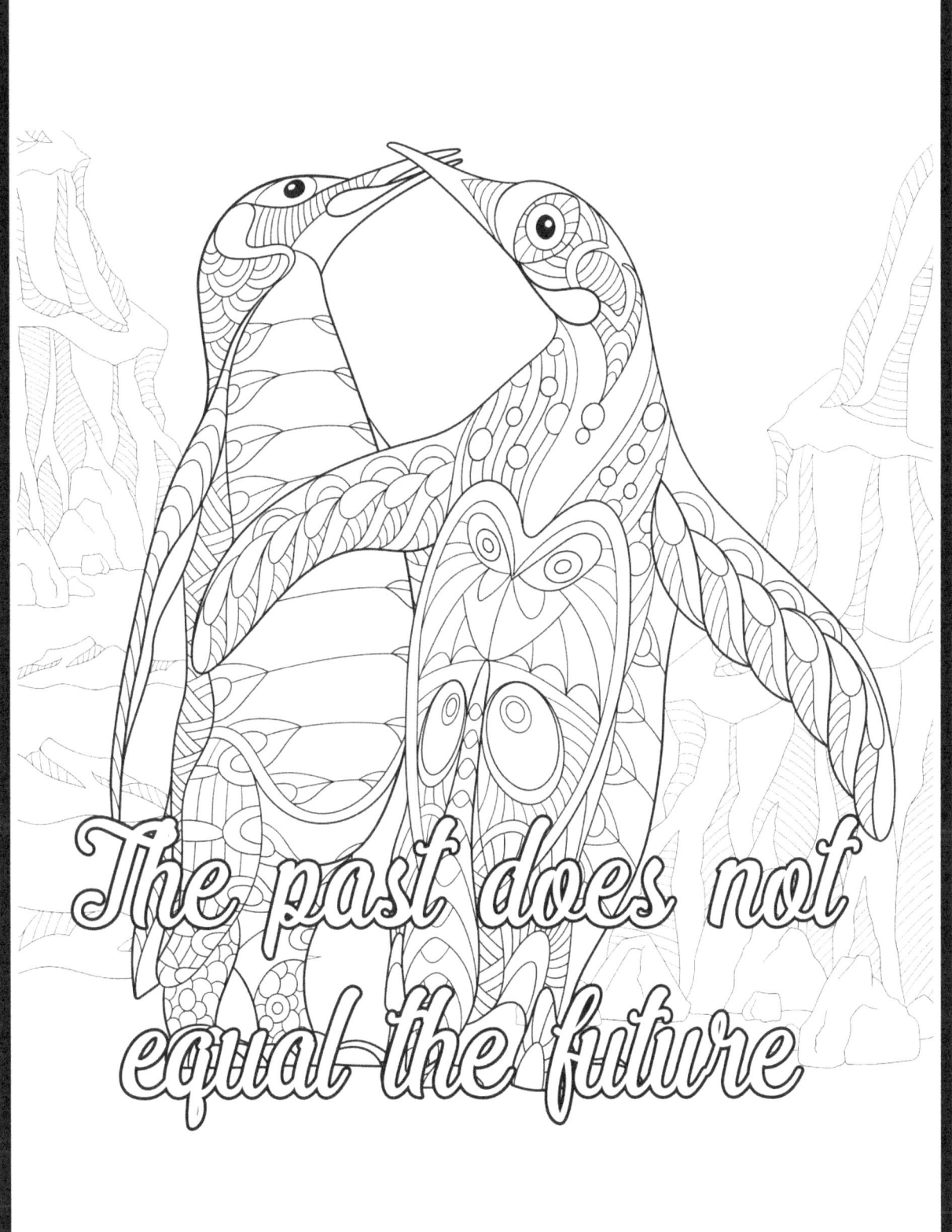

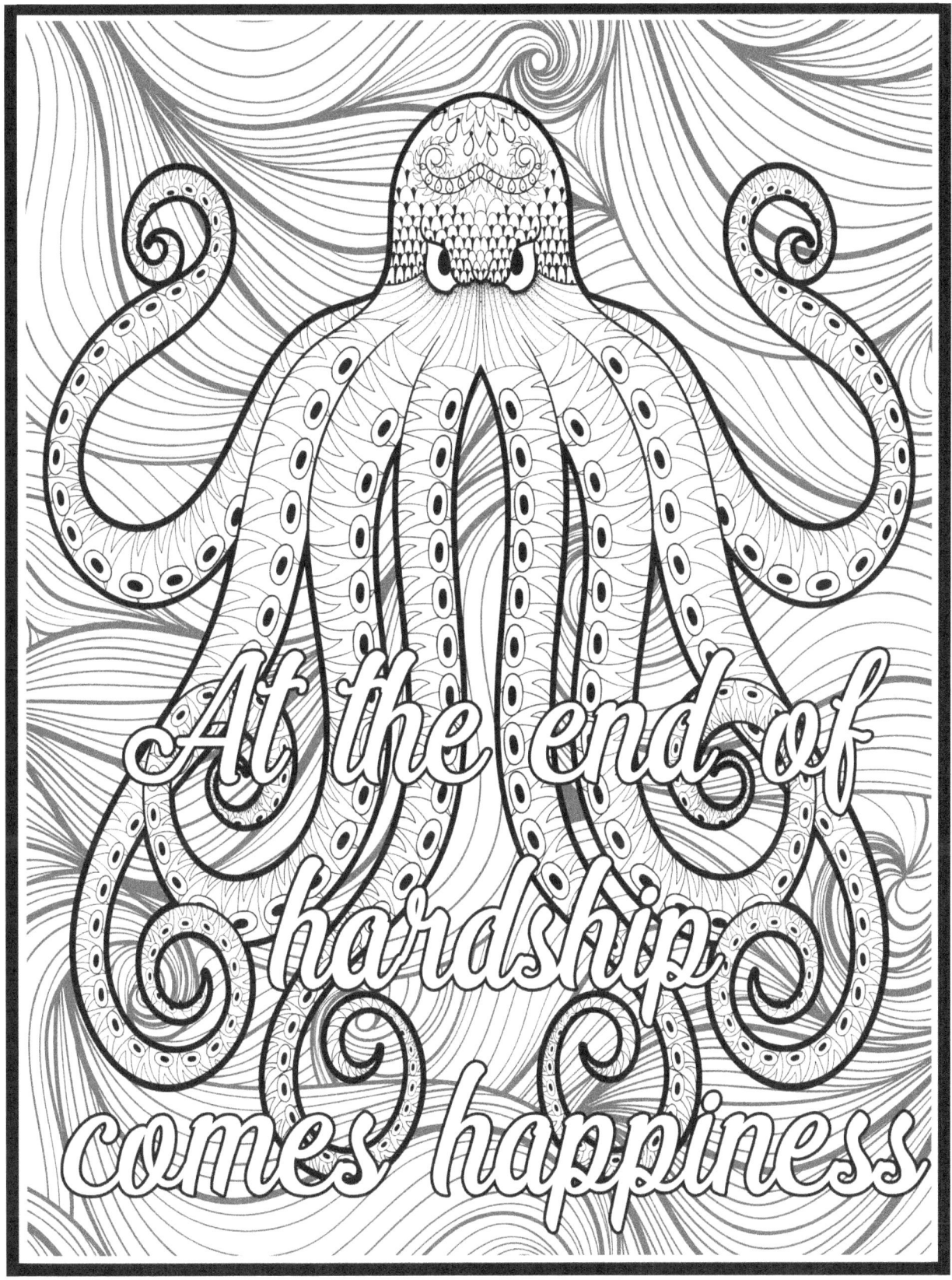

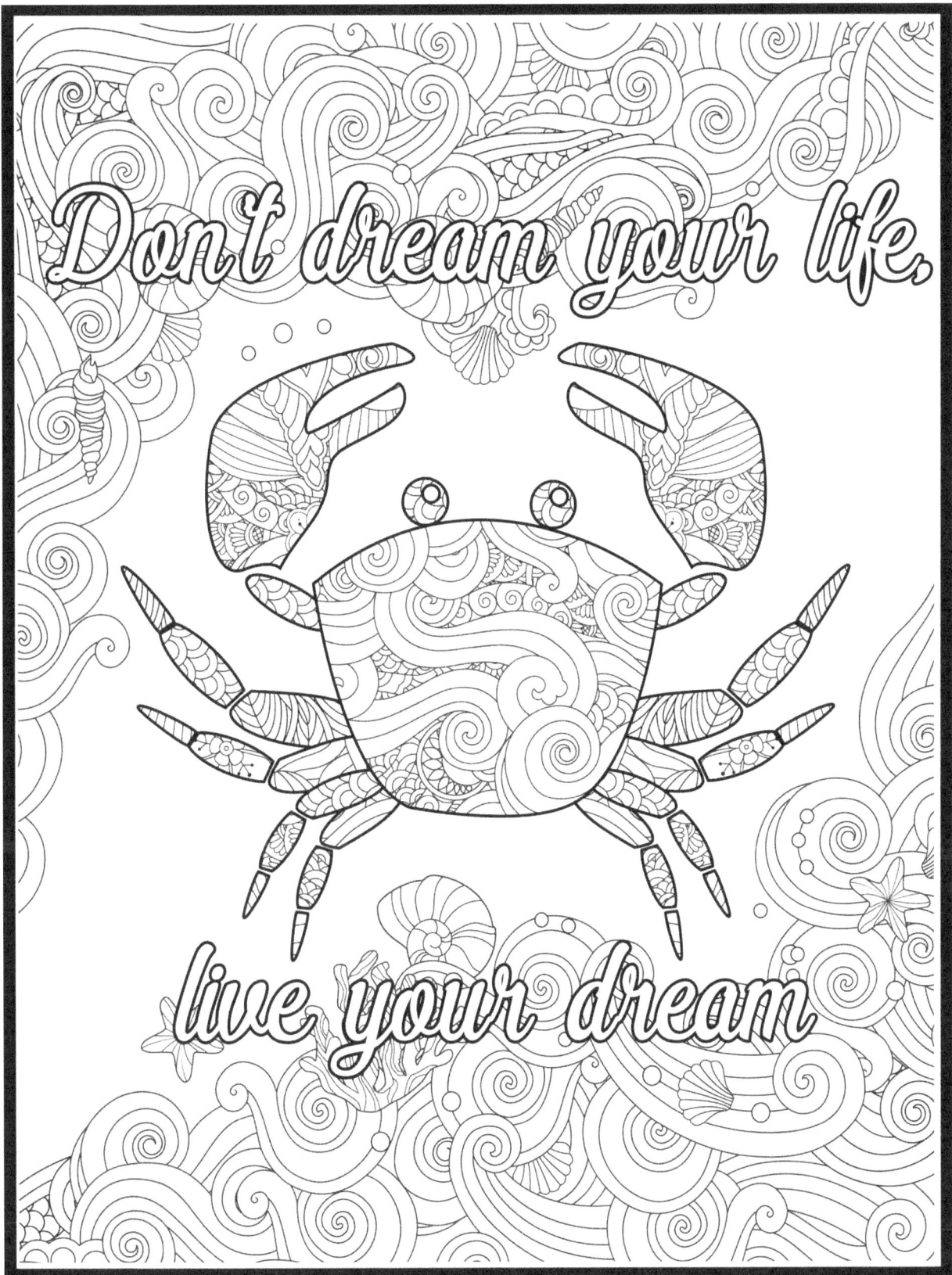

Dream without fear

Love without limits

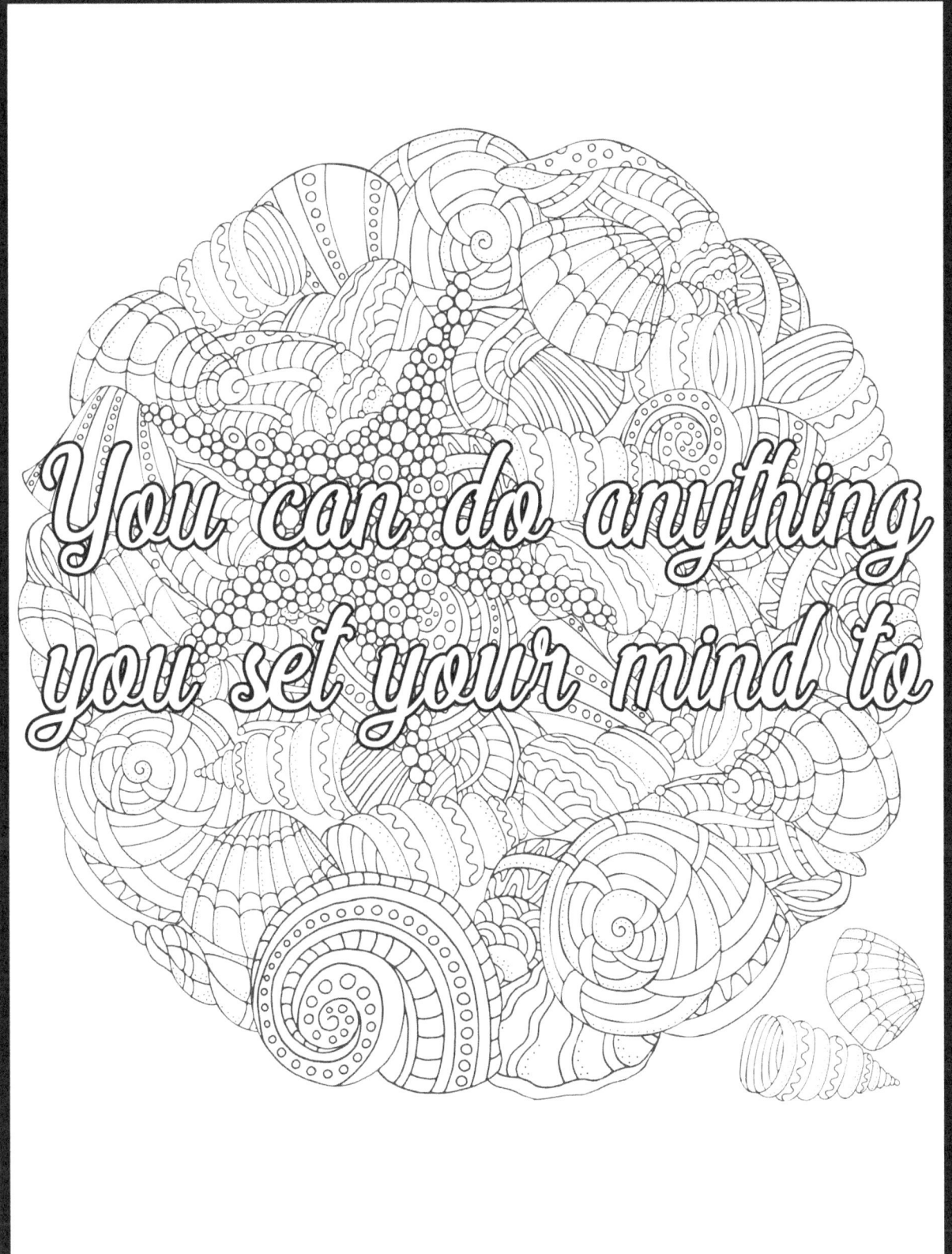

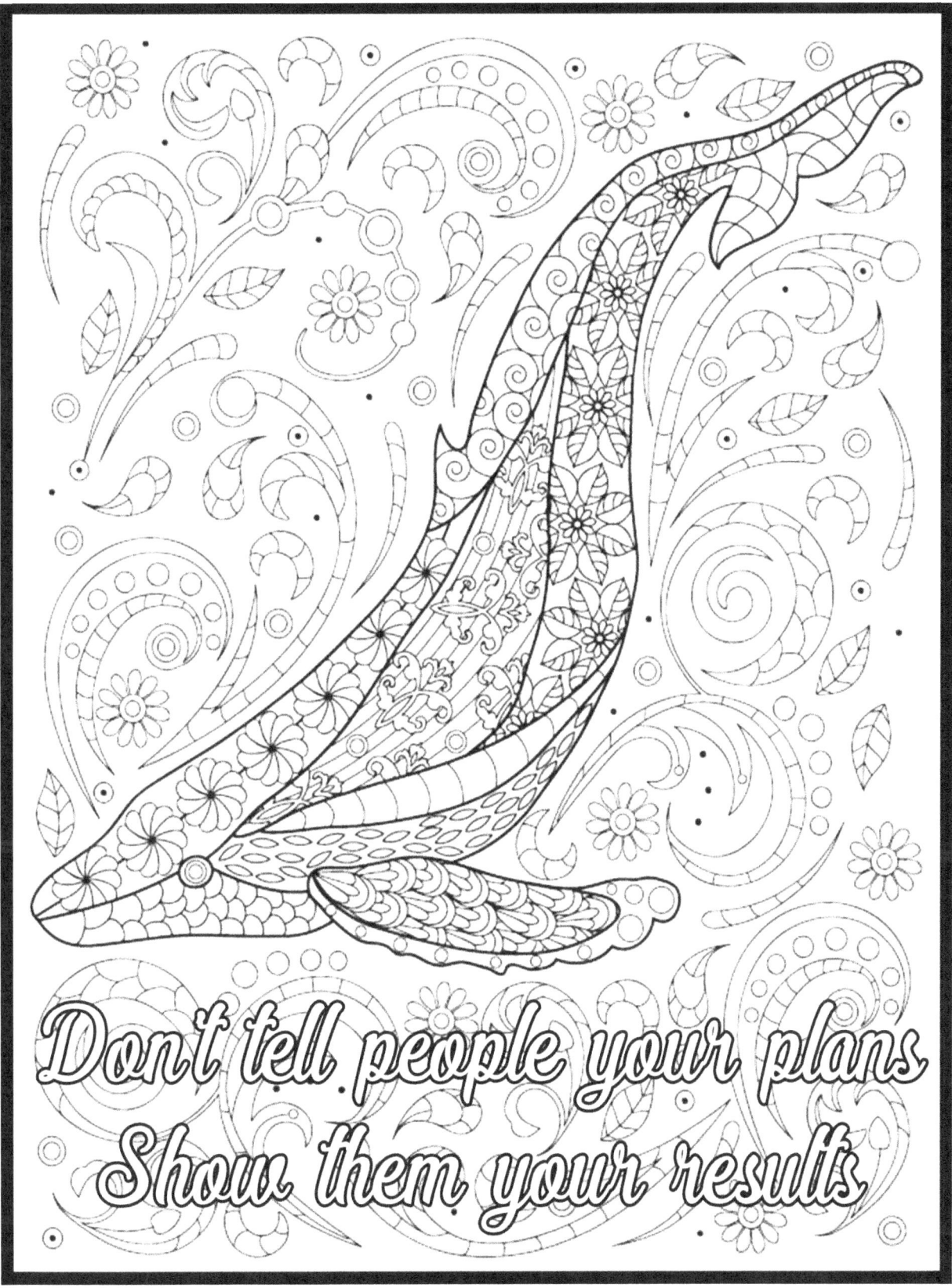

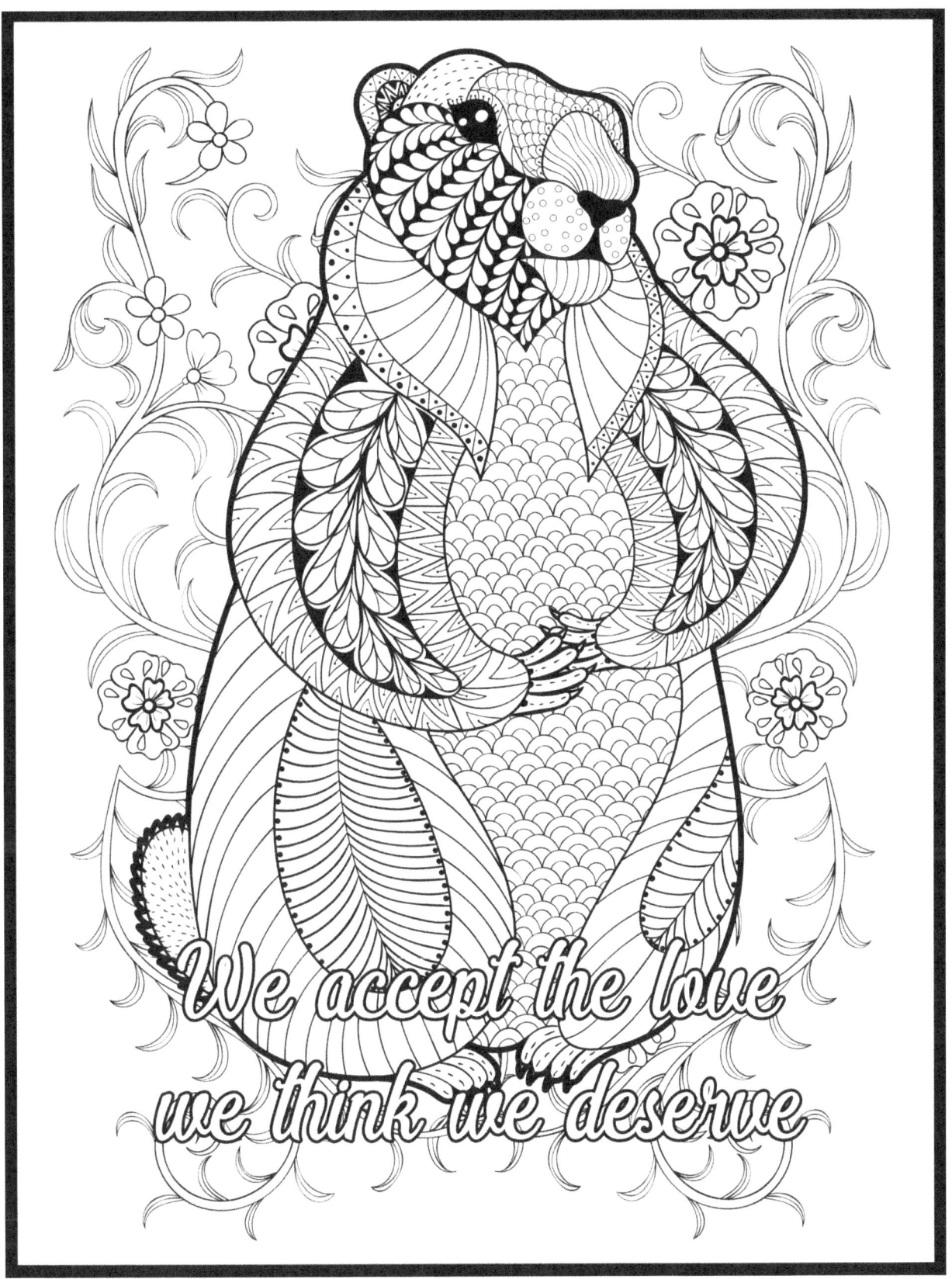

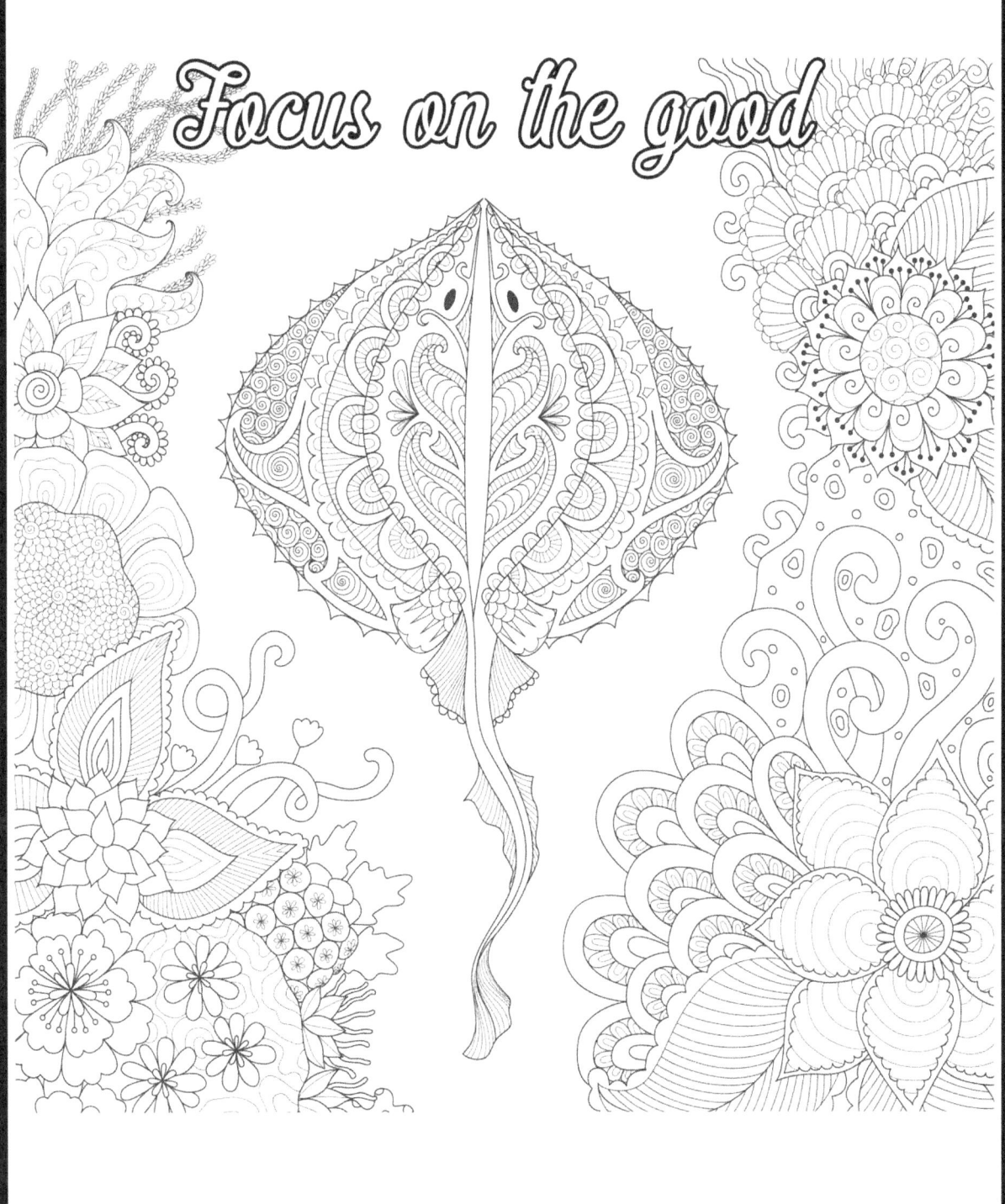

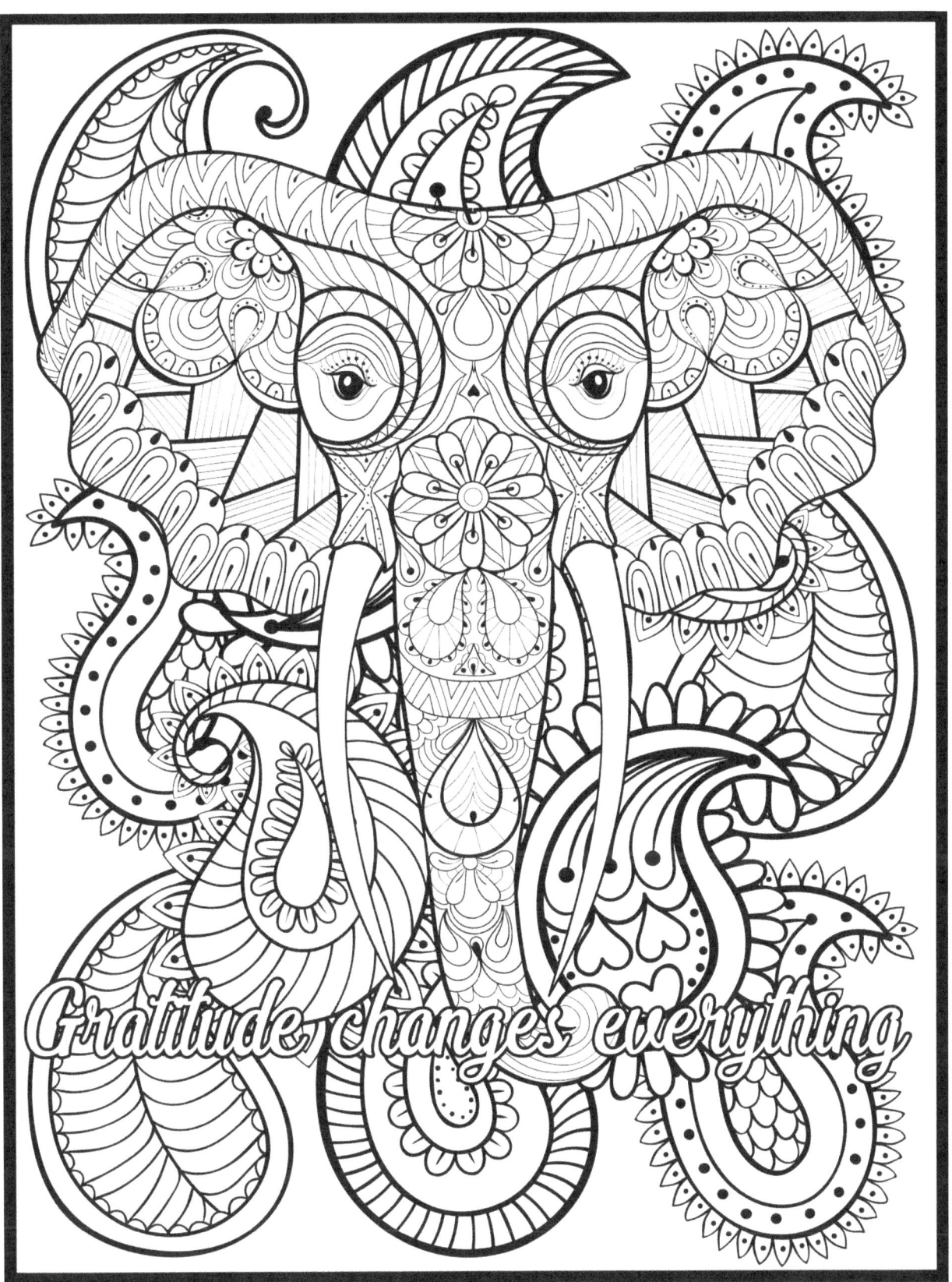

Thank you so much again for downloading this book! I hope you enjoyed coloring my book. Now I'd like ask for a *small* favor. Could you please take a minute or two and leave a review for this book. It'd be greatly appreciated! And I truly value your opinion and thoughts and I will incorporate them into my next book, which is already underway.

www.ingramcontent.com/pod-product-compliance
Lightning Source LLC
Chambersburg PA
CBHW082252220526
45469CB00009B/2974